More Praise for *The Fulles*

"Paul Chilcote has given us an irenic, detailed, and loving account of wny and now tne ways of Saint Benedict and the Wesleys are deeply convergent. Accessible and clear-headed, these pages guide the reader to a detailed understanding of these living spiritual traditions. Readers will find here both wisdom and resources for the Christian life. The nine patterns of vision and practice Chilcote develops—from 'attentiveness' to 'holiness'—are mutual treasures found in both these living traditions. As a result, we can truly say that the Benedictine ora et labora ('prayer and work') shines through in the sermons, prayers and hymns of the Wesleys. A fine achievement of ecumenical spiritual writing."
—Don E. Saliers, Wm. R. Cannon Distinguished Professor of Worship and Theology, Emeritus, Emory University, Atlanta, GA

"The Wesleys drank from deep wells to quench their thirst for spiritual nourishment. The Rule of Benedict was one of them. Combining the Rule with the Wesleyan way is just what we need to drink deeply ourselves."
—Steve Harper, retired seminary professor, speaker, and author

"*The Fullest Possible Love* is an engaging and profound reflection on common themes emerging within the Methodist/Wesleyan tradition and the Benedictine path. Chilcote explores the many ways the two approaches to Gospel living inform and strengthen each other, emphasizing such central practices as life together and the heart's ongoing formation. I find encouragement in Chilcote's sense of a fresh wind in the church today, coupled with his unabashed invitation to holiness!"
—Norvene Vest, Episcopal oblate of the Benedictine Sisters of Virginia, Bristow, VA

"In *The Fullest Possible Love*, Paul Chilcote explores Wesleyan and Benedictine spiritualities, offering insights into the quest for harmonious relationships with God and others. This book has helped me understand anew how to grow towards peace with myself, peaceful coexistence with others, and the flourishing of creation. Paul offers us a treasure trove of wisdom about the spiritual journey."
—Dion A. Forster, South African Methodist theologian; spiritual writer; and professor of Public Theology, Vrije Universiteit, Amsterdam, NL

"A friend once told me, after visiting our community, that he finally understood the purpose of monastic community: 'It makes it easier to be good.' In this volume we find the beautiful treasures of Benedictine spirituality alongside the animating energy of the Methodist movement, which in its own way was a 'new monastic' movement. This book is a treasure for all of us who seek to follow Christ in today's world."
—Elaine A. Heath, Abbess, The Church at Spring Forest, a new monastic community of the United Methodist tradition, Hillsborough, NC

"Paul Chilcote, a master teacher, invites Benedictines and Methodists to explore convergent themes grounded in spiritual practices. Mutual confidence in the possibility of Spirit-led growth in holy love is a place to begin! But as readers will discover, there is much more to savor in *The Fullest Possible Love!*"
—Michael Cartwright, emeritus associate professor, University of Indianapolis; author, *Watching Over One Another in Love: Reclaiming the Wesleyan Rule of Life for the Church's Mission*

"It is with joy and hope that I receive this latest book from Rev. Dr. Paul Chilcote, for it shares with the reader his long journey through the overlapping landscapes of the Methodist Way of Life and Benedictine monastic practices and wisdom. He is prepared to move gracefully through these overlaps, for he is a Methodist elder and a Benedictine oblate of Mount Angel Abbey, where I am currently the abbot. From my monastery I call down blessings on author and readers alike."

—Jeremy Driscoll, Abbot of Mount Angel Abbey, Saint Benedict, OR

"God's Spirit leaps from the pages of this book into the reader's own heart as this wholistic way of love is experienced both personally and for engagement within community. Each chapter invites prayerful wisdom from Scripture, St. Benedict, and the Wesley brothers."

—Brenda Buckwell, spiritual director and founder, Living Streams Flowing Water; author, *Spiritual Direction and the Metamorphosis of Church and The Advent of God's Word*

"In this thoughtful and engaging work, Paul Chilcote reminds us that Benedictine and Wesleyan hearts beat in a similar rhythm. They both offer an intentional and practical way of growing in the likeness of Christ, by God's grace. Chilcote rightly helps Methodism express its deeply embedded monastic voice for everyday followers of Jesus."

—Brett Opalinski, Assistant Dean of Methodist Studies, Candler School of Theology, Emory University, Atlanta, GA

"*The Fullest Possible Love* draws two great traditions of spiritual formation into dialogue with each other and into conversation with the reader through the experience and scholarship of Paul Chilcote. He draws the reader into visions of attentiveness, community, and harmony; practices of prayer, work, and sacred song; and goals of humility, hospitality, and holiness. This timely book demonstrates the true purpose, spirit, and fruit of ecumenical engagement."

—Jane Leach, principal, Wesley House Cambridge, Cambridge, UK; author, *A Charge to Keep: Reflective Supervision and the Renewal of Christian Leadership*

"*The Fullest Possible Love* will whet your appetite for a deeper, more intentional, vibrant life with Christ in community. Drawing from the deep wells of the Benedictine and Wesleyan traditions, Paul Chilcote explores their common visions, practices, and goals in the quest for peace with God and neighbor. Without wasting one word, he draws you toward a more contemplative way of praying and living."

—Trevor Hudson, lecturer; author, *Discovering Our Spiritual Identity and Invitations of Jesus*

"*The Fullest Possible Love* invites attentive and open-hearted engagement with the Benedictine and the Wesleyan spiritual traditions, and offers a contemporary vision of personal, relational and social transformation. This is a book to read and pray through, and a timely resource for the life of faith."

—Carole Irwin, British Methodist presbyter; research fellow, University of Aberdeen, Scotland

"'What do you seek?' That question is put before all who come to the Benedictine life. The answer to it means everything. This new work by Paul Chilcote will be a helpful companion for any reader endeavoring to sort out the many and various tangles that hinder one's search for clarity about desires of the heart. May we be led in its pages to the One we truly seek."

—Mary Ewing Stamps, Saint Brigid of Kildare Methodist-Benedictine Monastery, St. Joseph, MN

Paul W. Chilcote

The Fullest Possible Love

LIVING IN HARMONY
WITH GOD AND NEIGHBOR

Abingdon Press

Nashville

THE FULLEST POSSIBLE LOVE:
LIVING IN HARMONY WITH GOD AND NEIGHBOR

ISBN: 978-1-7910-3382-8
Library of Congress Control Number: 2024941017

MANUFACTURED IN THE UNITED STATES OF AMERICA

With gratitude for Benedict of Nursia,
Charles Wesley, and John Wesley,
for their vision of life in Christ
as the fullest possible love

– Contents –

Visit **abingdonpress.com/fullest-extra** to find an extra resource for this book:

> The Benedictine-Wesleyan way can be used to form new connections with people in a variety of settings, both inside and outside the church. A free, downloadable PDF provides step-by-step help for church leaders who want to teach or lead this new approach in their communities. This free resource is written by Michael Adam Beck.

Foreword

by Kenneth H. Carter

I live in the mountains of Western North Carolina and occasionally find myself hiking, often with friends more conversant with the surrounding ecosystem than I am. One of my favorite sections of the trail is an experience of convergence. It is the section where the Appalachian Trail joins the path explored by naturalist William Bartram in the 1770s, known as The Bartram Trail. It is clearly a single path, fifty-eight miles in length, with trail markers, shelters, and campsites here and there. But one travels this path fully aware that pilgrims before us carried different supplies, employed different habits, and read different signs in pursuit of their destinations. Yet it is one forest, one trail, one journey.

You are about to embark on a similar path, or perhaps you are well along in the journey. Here we discover a deep resonance in two living traditions, the Benedictine and the Wesleyan. And yet the two traditions tap into an even deeper well that is the mind of Christ, the accompanying Holy Spirit, the Creator God whose nature and name is Love.

Paul Chilcote has been on "a long obedience" in each of these communities, as a theologian, an ordained elder, an oblate, a disciple and and a pilgrim. He embodies the first and essential call in the Rule of Benedict—to listen. He listens to spiritual guides and theological mentors who are known and unknown to us; he listens to his own life; he listens for the voices of essential community and connection; and as a trained musician he also listens to the harmonies and dissonances that constitute the beauty of the gathered assembly.

In the best sense of his own Methodist ordination this is "practical divinity." And yet as one deeply rooted in history Paul understands that Methodism did not spring forth in a vacuum. This is the good soil of lives dedicated to the Triune God, grounded in covenantal obedience, in pursuit of a particular path whose destination is the most universal gift, the love of our Creator.

Throughout the history of the church there are upheavals and disruptions; in the first quarter of the twenty-first century, we have lived through acts of terrorism, a global pandemic, undeniable climate change, the rise of authoritarianism, and persistent divisions in the churches, Catholic, Protestant and Evangelical. Our way forward is a retrieval of this inheritance, the gift of traditions that converge in a beautiful and life-giving way.

To read this book is to find ourselves on the right path. It is to rejoice in faithful guides who have walked before us, Benedict and the Wesleys, and those who would follow in their paths. And now, in a providential moment, Paul Chilcote. Reading these pages, we are moved to take our next faithful steps, always listening and trusting, in the hopes that we are being renewed in the image of Christ by the One who loves us, and who desires the fullness of that love for each of us.

+ Kenneth H. Carter, Jr.
Resident Bishop, Western North Carolina Conference
The United Methodist Church

Foreword

by Odo Recker

Reading Paul Chilcote's reminiscences of the Robert Frost poem, "The Road Not Taken," I couldn't help but think about another Robert Frost poem that I often quote from, "Stopping by Woods on a Snowy Evening":

> *The woods are lovely, dark and deep,*
> *But I have promises to keep,*
> *And miles to go before I sleep,*
> *And miles to go before I sleep.*

The words remind me of unfinished business, which is how I see the way of conversion and growth in holiness. Without perseverance all our work can go for naught. Our relationship of love with Christ and our brothers and sisters in Christ can be *lovely and deep,* but we cannot imagine we are 'finished.' *I have promises to keep.* My baptismal promises and religious vows are for life, just as marriage vows are for life. As long as I live there will always be *miles to go before I sleep.*

The Wesleyan and Benedictine ways do converge *in the wood,* and each can help the other as they cover the *miles before they sleep.* The promises Paul Chilcote made as a Benedictine Oblate have aided him in being a faithful and successful Methodist, pastor, and theologian. This pathway to holiness in community has been trod for fifteen hundred years; it serves as a model for success in many endeavors. Paul's experience and his research, both evident in this book, demonstrate this point.

The energy in a community of monks and oblates carries tremendous power to transform ourselves and our world according to the mind of Christ. Our *spiritual communion* in prayer and work multiplies our individual efforts and opens us up to a power beyond ourselves. An oblate of a community of Benedictine monks or nuns can draw on the strength of the community. I urge you, reader, to consider what this might mean for you.

One might assume only Catholics are permitted to become a Benedictine Oblate, but this is not so. The community of which I'm a part, Mount Angel, is happy to have Oblates of other Christian traditions. As explained on our website, www.mountangelabbey.org:

> Oblates of Mount Angel Abbey seek God in Christian Discipleship in the world. By obedience, faithfulness to prayer and continual conversion of life according to the Holy Rule of Saint Benedict, oblates seek union with God and growth in charity toward one's neighbor. . . .
>
> Oblates of Saint Benedict are Christians who have experienced in some way a call to embrace Benedictine spirituality. After a time of prayer and discernment they make a more formal, permanent commitment to a monastic community. By making this formal self-giving to Christ in communion with a monastic community, the oblate embraces the time-tested traditions and values of the Benedictine way. Oblates are united to the prayer and good works of the monastery to which they are associated while they continue to live out their Christian vocation in the world.

In reading this book you will see how the Benedictine Way and the Wesleyan Way converge. I hope you might also consider a call to become a Benedictine oblate yourself. It is a way we can "become one" in Christ even though the reality of separation still exists. May we Methodists and Catholics continue to converge until we can be One in Communion at the Table of the Lord.

Father Odo Recker, O.S.B.
Director of Monastic Vocations
Mt. Angel Abbey

Preface

I memorized Robert Frost's famous poem "The Road Not Taken" as many in my generation did, when I was in high school.[1] Singing Randall Thompson's choral setting around that same time further imprinted the words and images on my mind. With those opening words, "Two roads diverged in a yellow wood," Frost provides a parable about life. He invites us into the age-old story of a juncture in the road and the decision forced upon each of us in that moment. Which way do I take?

But there is another way to look at that path. It all depends on your destination—the direction of your journey—doesn't it? Instead of a divergence, you could equally view it, from the opposite direction, as a convergence. If you are walking in the opposite direction, the two roads force no decision; rather, they merge and continue in a new, singular path. This different view of the scene also opens the possibility of a relational image. Think of two people walking on each of the different forks of the road toward each other in such a way that they meet at the juncture. The convergence offers an opportunity to journey together as companions. This book is about the convergence of two roads. "Two roads converged," I want to say, "in a yellow wood." One of those roads is the Benedictine way; the other is the Wesleyan way.

One of the reasons I think about Frost's scene in this way is because these two roads converged in my own life. This convergence, in fact, defines my own spiritual journey. I found myself as a traveler on both

---

1. See Robert Frost, "A Group of Poems," *The Atlantic*, 1915, https://www.theatlantic.com/magazine/archive/1915/08/a-group-of-poems/306620/, accessed March 6, 2023.

paths. I grew up with deep roots in Methodism, that Protestant tradition tracing its spiritual lineage back to John and Charles Wesley in England. I used to say that if you cut me, I would bleed Methodist blood. My grandfather served as a Methodist pastor. My father served as a Methodist pastor. I also felt called into the Methodist ministry, after a fairly intense period of discernment.

I love my Methodist heritage. I love its emphasis on the necessity of translating faith into action. I love its vision of discipleship as faith working by love leading to holiness of heart and life. It is little wonder that, after ordination, I made the decision to pursue further study of the Wesleyan tradition and its founders, in particular, completing my doctoral studies in early British Methodism and the wide space it gave to women in the movement. I understand my spiritual life—my relationship with God—primarily through a Wesleyan lens. That is the spiritual path I've been on the longest, but it has never been the only path to beckon me onward and upward.

I will never forget the day my father and uncle took my brother and me to visit a Benedictine monastery in southern Indiana. We were visiting my aunt, uncle, and cousins in Boonville where my uncle, Howard Ellis, pastored the local Methodist church. Saint Meinrad Archabbey was just about a forty-five-minute drive and Howdy, as he was known by his friends, was eager for us to see the magnificent church there. We simply made a day of it. I must have been around eight years of age. This was my first time to visit a monastery. I just remember being enthralled. My favorite part of the day was joining the monks for evening prayer. My first viewing of the mural of Christ—the Christus—in the apse of the Archabbey Church overwhelmed me. I could not take my eyes off it throughout the vespers service, in part, because Jesus never seemed to take his eyes off me.

I loved the quiet, the rhythmic shuffle of the monks' feet as they made their way into the choir, the chanting, the prayers, the peace. That impression has never faded. I knew, even at that tender age, I was something of a contemplative, although I had no vocabulary for it. My mother had always referred to me as "pondering Paul," and the monastery impressed me as a place where a person like me could feel at home. After we returned to our home in the Chicago area, on the following

Sunday, in his morning sermon, my father told the congregation about our visit to St. Meinrad. He painted a portrait of the community, its common life, and its ongoing rhythm of work and prayer. He reverently concluded, "Whenever people hear the bells ringing from the tower of the abbey church, they know that devout disciples of Jesus are turning to God in prayer."

Fast-forward some thirty years. In 1994 I was teaching at Africa University in Zimbabwe. I received an invitation to participate in the first, and up to this point only, international joint Methodist and Benedictine conference. The theme of this event was "Sanctification in the Benedictine and Methodist Traditions."[2] The organizers encouraged me to contribute an essay on that theme through the lens of early Methodist women—a topic upon which I had already done some publishing. The time I spent at Mondo Migliori, Rocca di Papa, just outside Rome, rubbing shoulders and sharing ideas with monastics and scholars, reignited my interest in the Benedictine tradition as never before. But this renewed interest really came through an unexpected, personal connection more than anything else.

One of the participants, a young British woman, looked extremely familiar to me, but I just couldn't place her. After several days of searching my memory to no avail, I greeted her and told her my name. "Oh my goodness," she squealed. "I am Linda Wisheart. The little girl you knew in Bristol." In the early 1980s my family and I had lived in Westbury-on-Trym under the auspices of a Rotary International Fellowship with the University of Bristol. Linda was the daughter of the family who had adopted us as new visitors of the local Methodist church. "What has brought you here?" I asked. She explained to me that she was a Benedictine oblate.[3]

---

2. The papers from this conference were subsequently published as *Sanctification in the Benedictine and Wesleyan Traditions: A World Ecumenical Conference, July 7–10, 1994* (Wilmore, KY: First Fruits Press, 2015).

3. Benedictine Oblates are followers of Jesus who associate with a particular Benedictine community to enrich their Christian way of life. They follow the Rule of St. Benedict as closely as they can within the context of their own status in life and without formal monastic vows. By integrating their life of prayer and work, they seek to lives Christ's presence in the world. See http://www.archive.osb.org/obl/intro .html, accessed March 13, 2023.

I had never heard of this before. So I thoroughly interrogated her about what it meant to be an oblate and how she had come to invest her life in this kind of relationship with Downside Abbey, just south of Bristol, near the great cathedral city of Wells. Her story—really her testimony—fascinated me. Once back in the United States after bidding farewell to Zimbabwe later that summer, I simply shelved all these discoveries. My family and I were too distant from any Benedictine community where we lived at that time for me to be able to do anything about the internal nudges I felt.

An unexpected opportunity to explore what being an oblate might mean soon emerged. In 1995–96 a door opened for me to do some entrepreneurial work related to theological education when I was on the faculty at the Methodist Theological School in Ohio. Kempton Hewitt, the dean at the time and a native of the Pacific Northwest, was concerned about the dearth of Christian influence in that area of the country. He birthed the idea of a House of Theological Studies out in that region and invited me to pioneer this work with him. Our base of operations for this exciting work was Mount Angel Abbey in Oregon.

I first stepped foot on the grounds of this monastic community set on a hill on July 6, 1996. I remember so clearly the winding drive up the gentle hillside, passing the stations of the cross along the roadside, and catching sight of the abbey church at the top of the hill. I have no other way to explain my experience other than to say, as soon as I arrived there, I felt like I had come home. It was a busy two weeks with teaching daily, preaching, and sightseeing on the weekends. But more than anything else, for the first time in my life, I had the opportunity to experience the patterns and rhythms of a Benedictine community at prayer and work. I fell in love with it all.

Father Odo Recker was responsible for the hospitality afforded our group, and he and I became fast friends. I talked with him about the possibility of becoming an oblate of the abbey and he arranged a time for me to meet with Father Bernard Sanders, the director of oblates. He had me at hello. I'm not really sure what kind of image I had in mind before actually meeting the monks of the abbey in the context of their own life and work, but Father Bernard personified the grace, wisdom, and gentleness I suppose I expected.

He had a way of putting a person at ease, and we talked together for some time, quietly and effortlessly. My main questions revolved around what the expectations might be for a non-Catholic, married, and quite distant member of the community. He put all my concerns to rest. Even as I write now, his grace and the love he exuded stand out above all other things. Father Bernard's every word spoke "welcome." When I asked about expectations related to my life of prayer, he said quite simply that his hope was for me to pray regularly each day. I said, "I can do that." And then he added, speaking slowly and deliberately, "And a good place to start would be the Psalms." He closed our time together with an eloquent prayer and invited me to undergo a one-year novitiate with the hopes of my making my oblation the following July when I had planned to return. Once back in Ohio, I began a systematic study of St. Benedict's Rule with the help of Norvene Vest's excellent workbook *Preferring Christ.*[4]

Truth be told, my life of prayer changed very little, since I had already dedicated myself to a fairly consistent pattern of Morning Prayer, at least, using the service of the Anglican tradition. But my life of prayer felt more focused. I no longer felt that I was alone in prayer. I felt buoyed up by an unseen community. That sense of solidarity grew over the year, despite the miles that separated me physically from the abbey. I could still hear the sound of the bells—the "voice of God" as they would say—summoning me away from the rush of life into the calming reality of God's presence. The following year, on July 31, 1997, the feast day of St. Ignatius Loyola, with Father Odo and my dear friend and fellow oblate, Nikki Martin, at my side, I made my final oblation and became an oblate of Mount Angel Abbey. I took the name "Bede," the venerable English Benedictine saint I had long admired. I told Father Bernard after the ceremony that I now felt rooted in something ancient, deep, and enduring.

Two roads converged. No sudden wrenching of the gears. No sharp turn requiring guard rails or danger signs. To change the image, this was just a calm confluence of the Benedictine and the Wesleyan

---

4. Norvene Vest, *Preferring Christ: A Devotional Commentary on the Rule of Saint Benedict* (New York: Morehouse Publishing, 2004).

streams of my life. Two streams, two paths, merged into one. In the intervening twenty-five years I have had many opportunities to reflect on the meaning of these events in my life. What I have discovered—as many of us had at that joint conference in Rome—is a deep resonance. In this book I share the insights I've gained and the lessons I've learned on this journey. I explore a Benedictine Wesleyan way that, I believe, can lead to spiritual vitality and peace—abundant life—for anyone.

Paul Wesley "Bede" Chilcote, OblSB

Acknowledgments

Both the Benedictine and Wesleyan traditions value community. They have taught me to value it as well. Publishing a book involves multiple communities. Authors are never islands unto themselves. Despite the fact I typed words into a word processor at the front end of this process, innumerable colleagues and friends turned that manuscript into this book. I am grateful to everyone who played a part along the way.

In order to honor both the Benedictine and Wesleyan communities that have shaped me and this book, I wanted to have a Foreword, if possible, from representatives of each tradition. So I appreciate the ways in which Bishop Ken Carter and Father Odo Recker have so carefully prepared statements that provide a gateway to this journey you are taking.

I appreciate every endorsement, of course, but the statements of four special people to me mean a great deal. Jeremy Driscoll is the abbot of my monastic home, Mt. Angel Abbey in Oregon. Norvene Vest is a Benedictine oblate, whose many publications on the spiritual life continue to shape my understanding of this unique calling. Don Saliers is a United Methodist Benedictine oblate and theologian of the church who is such a kindred spirit. Mary Ewing Stamps is the founder of St. Brigid of Kildare monastery, which is the only Methodist community built on the Benedictine model that I am aware of in the world. To these four fellow sojourners, many, many thanks.

As I worked on this project, I invited a number of friends to read chapters as they fell into place. Several people took my invitation very seriously, and their comments have improved this book in many ways. Thanks in this regard to Brenda Buckwell, Steve Harper, Elaine Heath,

Trevor Hudson, Sharon Rowland, and Mary Ewing Stamps. Michael Beck is preparing a special guide for Fresh Expressions communities to be used alongside this book, so special thanks to him for this labor of love.

The staff at Abingdon Press are fantastic. Many thanks to Neil Alexander for his early encouragement, and Connie Stella and Katie Johnston for their editorial expertise.

As always, a final word of thanks to my beloved, Janet, for her patience with me when, as she would say, I am on my book train. She is more precious to me than I can ever say and the inspiration behind everything I do.

Signposts and Instructions for the Journey

When you prepare to embark on a journey, it is always helpful to be aware of signposts along the way and to have some basic instructions in hand. The journey ahead of you here is not complex. My hope, however, is that it will be profound for you. These two paths—the Benedictine and the Wesleyan—are well trod. Thousands of pilgrims have made the journey into a deeper awareness of God and God's love following these paths. But your journey is yours and yours alone, or better put, a journey made with your own companions who are seeking the same goal in life. The first signpost says the best way to make this journey is in the company of others. Taking this journey with friends will enhance it, so I suggest that you make this a community adventure.

The second signpost has to do with the content. You will note immediately from this book's table of contents alone that there is a certain order here. I explain this organization of ideas and practices in the introduction. So there is a flow, so to speak, that is derived from these two paths. Having said that, however, you need not travel through this book by strict sequence. The chapters are self-contained. So follow the leading of the Spirit in terms of how you navigate the material. You may be drawn naturally to some topics by virtue of your interest or because of the novelty to you personally or as a group. In whatever way you decide to read through this book, the destination remains the same—a deeper connection with and experience of God's love for you.

Some books are meant to be read through quickly. This one is not. The third signpost says take you time. Pause. Ponder. Reflect. Write. Think of this journey as a devotional practice in and of itself. Use this time to practice the presence of God and to enhance your awareness of God's place in your life. In his classic book *The Sacrament of the Present Moment*, Jean Pierre de Caussade says that we should read quietly, slowly, word for word to enter into the subject more with the heart than the mind.[1] Many people find journaling to be a helpful way to collect your reflections. I encourage you to keep a journal of your spiritual experience or to create opportunities for you to share your reflections with others as you travel together.

At the close of each chapter, I provide three resources (I call them treasures) to encourage your deeper engagement with a Benedictine Wesleyan way of living your faith. Here are a few instructions concerning their use.

Over the years I have developed my own particular form of *lectio divina* (sacred reading) that I practice regularly. It draws upon several different sources including the basic template of Teresian *lectio* and Salesian or Anglican meditation.[2] At the conclusion of each chapter, I invite you into this simple form of contemplative reflection that has come to mean so much to me. I provide a specific scripture text for you to reflect upon related to the topic of the chapter. I call each of these "A Biblical Treasure." One of the keys to a meaningful experience of spiritual or sacred reading, in my view, is permitting the text to read you instead of you reading the text. Rather than turning a passage of scripture into an object to be studied or analyzed, the purpose is to permit God to speak to you through it, to guide, instruct, and restore you. This creates space for an awareness of God's presence. This is a marvelous way to bring religious texts to life, for scripture to become the living Word for you and your community.

Like most forms of *lectio divina*, my own practice moves successively through four movements. Four simple words—proclaim, picture, ponder, practice—provide the framework for this reflective or meditative engagement with the texts. Before you begin, I strongly recommend that you take some time to relax, breathe deeply, center

---

1. See Jean Pierre de Caussade, *The Sacrament of the Present Moment*, trans. Kitty Muggeridge (San Francisco: HarperSanFrancisco, 1966).
2. In chapter 1 I explain these more fully.

yourself, and invite the Holy Spirit to direct your reading and reflection. Be assured that God is always with you. Indeed, God has brought you to this moment and envelopes you with the love of Christ through the power of the Spirit. But it is right to invite the Triune God into the experience as you begin with a prayer. It can be as simple as this: "Speak to me, loving God, for your servant is ready to listen."

Having prepared yourself to spend this time intentionally with God, here are some practical instructions related to each of the four steps.

Proclaim. Read the passage. It is not essential, but I recommend that you read it out loud. It is important for us to actually hear the Word "proclaimed." After you have completed this first reading, spend a few moments in silence and let the words and images wash over you.

Picture. Read the same text through again, this time picturing yourself somewhere in the narrative. Where are you in the scene? What is your role? What are your feelings about all you have heard and seen? With which person do you identify? Again, spend a few moments in silence as you continue to imaginatively "compose the scene" and your place in the unfolding story.

Ponder. After a third reading of the text, ponder what these words might mean for you today. Why do your heart and mind dwell on particular aspects of the narrative? Are there any words or phrases that linger? How might God be speaking to you through these words? What insight have you gained about God, your neighbor, and yourself? What significance do you attach to your discoveries given your recent experiences, relationships, or concerns? Continue in this mode of pondering as long as it feels right to you. Enjoy this time spent with God in silent dialogue as God speaks to your heart.

Practice. Following a final reading of the passage, resolve to translate your insights and discoveries in the meditation into concrete actions. What is God calling you to do with this today? What action is required? What words need to be shared with others? What does God require of you to be an ambassador of reconciliation and love throughout the course of the day?

Proclaim—Picture—Ponder—Practice

Conclude the *lectio* experience with a brief prayer of gratitude to God. You began with God in prayer. Now, as you bring closure to this special time, think of this concluding prayer not so much as an ending as a beginning. As you live into God's vision, seek to be faithful to the Word proclaimed, pictured, pondered, and now practiced. I invite you into this *lectio divina* process as a concluding practice at the close of each chapter.

You will find two other resources at the conclusion of each chapter that I call "A Benedictine Treasure" and "A Wesleyan Treasure." The former are all prayers by Benedictine authors or used somewhat typically in the context of Benedictine communities; the latter are all excerpts from hymns written by Charles Wesley. With regard to both of these additional resources, feel free to apply the *lectio divina* process I have just outlined for you. On the other hand, you may simply wish to read and ponder each prayer and each hymn. If there is a "pause" before you move on to the next chapter you read, you may consider rereading the prayer and/or hymn daily.

My hope is that God will bless you with a rich treasury of spiritual insight through these additional resources. They provide an opportunity for you to embed your life more fully in the biblical, Benedictine, and Wesleyan vision of life in Christ. My prayer is that, through these exercises, you will experience God's love, be transformed by it, and grow into the most loving person you can be in this life.

Introduction

The Benedictine and Wesleyan traditions of Christian spirituality hold so much in common. In the course of these past twenty-five years, as these two paths have converged into one for me personally, so many points of connection have leaped out at me along the way. Some are obvious. Others are more nuanced. But when these two ways are held together, I believe the convergence offers a compelling vision of life in Christ rooted in love.

A Benedictine Wesleyan way begins with an acknowledgment of the realities of life. It starts where you are. It is neither heroic nor pedestrian; it is real. It does not shape you into someone so heavenly minded that you are no earthly good. It is not a "pie in the sky by and by" version of discipleship that leaves you frustrated or disillusioned on the pathway. Ecstasy and agony punctuate real life, with a whole lot of ordinary in the in-between times. This way of following Christ offers the same mountaintops and valleys, with practices that help you celebrate the victories, learn from the defeats, and sustain you along the way.

The pilgrimage, like any valuable or worthwhile quest leading from a point of beginning to a goal, entails struggles and challenges. It also offers healing, encouragement, and restoration. A Benedictine Wesleyan way, essentially, is a quest for the fullest possible love of God and neighbor in real time in this life. Love and grace motivate the journey. God envelops you with love and grace each step of the way. Love and grace draw you onward and upward toward the genuine purpose of your life, which is love.

Two roads converged. I have found this convergent way to be life-giving. For those of you who are not familiar with the Benedictine

1

tradition, my intention is to provide enough information to create a living portrait of this way. My approach is the same for those who know little about the Wesleyan way. My ultimate hope revolves more around the formational aspects of these traditions rather than information about them. I leave whatever transformation you may experience to the activity of the Holy Spirit. In this introduction, then, I invite you to explore this way with me, first, by briefly examining the life of St. Benedict, his Rule, and his way. Then I will introduce you to John and Charles Wesley, their General Rules, and their way. Finally, we'll reflect together on the convergent, salient themes that shape a Benedictine Wesleyan way—the path to spiritual vitality and peace.

The Benedictine Way

Benedict of Nursia (c. 480–547) lived in an age of transition characterized by chaos in both church and society.[1] Having aligned itself with the Roman Empire, the church found itself in a precarious position as the social structures to which it was bound disintegrated around it. One wave of Germanic migration after another—the so-called Barbarian invasions—left the fragile empire gasping for survival. Born into this fragmented and disorienting world, Benedict left very little behind for us to piece together anything other than a skeletal framework of his life. Only two sources provide insight into how he related to this world, but they do give us a clear idea of what he understood his calling and mission to be in it.

Pope Gregory the Great's *Dialogues*, written about fifty years after Benedict's death on March 21, 547, offer the only biographical account of this entrepreneurial monastic leader.[2] Gregory devotes the

---

1. I heartily recommend as an introduction to his life and work, Anselm Grün, *Benedict of Nursia: His Message for Today*, trans. Linda M. Maloney (Collegeville, MN: Liturgical Press, 2006). See also Columba Stewart, *Prayer and Community: The Benedictine Tradition*, ed. Philip Sheldrake, Traditions of Christian Spirituality (Maryknoll, NY: Orbis Books, 1998).

2. See Gregory the Great, *The Dialogues of Gregory the Great*, ed. and trans. Myra L. Uhlfelder, book 2, *Saint Benedict* (Indianapolis: Bobbs-Merrill, 1967). This account is a complex mixture of historical facts and legendary narratives circulating among the immediate successors of Benedict.

entire Second Book to Benedict's life and mission of spiritual renewal. He wanted to illustrate "God at work in [a] man's life," claims Esther de Waal. "He illustrates the law of paradox; genuine fruitfulness comes from what at first seems sterile; life come out of death."[3] Born in Umbrian Nursia around 480, Benedict spent several years in the imperial capital as a student of law and rhetoric. Disillusioned by some of his discoveries in Rome, however, he abandoned everything, embracing a life of solitude in the caves of Subiaco, east of the city. His journey from solitude to life in community was rather tortuous. But recognizing his spiritual depth, Christian ascetics in the area turned to Benedict to provide leadership for their fledgling communities. In his work with these fellow monastics he gained insight by trial and error into the nature and needs of those bound together in Christ.

The great turning point came for Benedict when he founded a monastic community on the mountain above Cassino around 529. By this time he not only had a wealth of experience as a spiritual guide but had also immersed himself in the nascent monastic traditions of both Eastern and Western Christianity. The consolidation of these various approaches to the spiritual life in community became his driving passion. He believed deeply that this was the way to deeper love of God and others. This new community under this direction began to thrive. "In a world prey to violence and famine," as Lin Donnat observes, "the monastery was an island of humanity where all men were welcome, barbarians and slaves alongside the descendants of noblemen. . . . Monte Cassino was a place of peace, a centre of prayer, a haven of culture."[4] Scholastica, who may have been his twin, resonated with his vision and founded her own community of women nearby. Benedict remained in his monastery atop the mountain the rest of his life.[5] Here

3. Esther de Waal, *Seeking God: The Way of St. Benedict* (Collegeville, MN: Liturgical Press, 1984), 17.

4. Lin Donnat, "St. Benedict and His Rule," in *Saint Benedict of Nursia: A Way of Wisdom for Today*, ed. A. Borias et al. (Strasbourg: Édition du Signe, 1994), 5.

5. For information on the life and work of St. Scholastica, see Mary Richard Boo and Joan M. Braun, "Emerging from the Shadows: St Scholastica," in *Medieval Women Monastics: Wisdom's Wellsprings*, ed. Miriam Schmitt and Linda Kulzer (Collegeville, MN: Liturgical Press, 1996), 1–11.

he wrote his Rule to provide a template of discipleship for those who sought to follow Christ in community.

Benedict's Rule—the second source of information about his life—provides deeper insight into who he was as a spiritual leader and guide.[6] The Rule itself provides a portrait, not only of the community the author sought "to establish as a school for the Lord's service" (RB Prol.45), but of the founder as someone captured by "the inexpressible sweetness of love" (RB Prol.49).

In one of her commentaries on the Rule, Sister Joan Chittister makes an important distinction between a law (*lex*) and a rule (*regula*).[7] The Rule is not a set of demands to be obeyed compulsively or obsessively; rather, it is a guide, a way or "rule of life." As a rule of life it sets your course, reminds you about those things that really matter, and fixes your attention on the goal you are pursuing together. Stephen Macchia views Benedict's Rule in this light:

> A rule of life is a set of guidelines that support or enable us to do the things we want and need to do. A rule of life allows us to clarify our deepest values, our most important relationships, our most authentic hopes and dreams, our most meaningful work, our highest priorities. It allows us to live with intention and purpose in the present moment. . . . A rule is like a trellis which offers support and guidance for a plant, helping it to grow in a certain direction.[8]

As such, the Rule has been a guide to the spiritual life for ordinary people who, as Sister Joan likes to say, are seeking to live extraordinarily well.

---

6. See the definitive edition of the Rule, St. Benedict, *RB1980 The Rule of St. Benedict in Latin and English with Notes*, ed. Timothy Fry et al. (Collegeville, MN: Liturgical Press, 1981), which I have collated with Judith Sutera, ed., *St. Benedict's Rule: An Inclusive Translation* (Collegeville, MN: Liturgical Press, 2021), the edition quoted throughout. This Fry text is generally referred to as RB1980. Parenthetically inserted references from Sutera follow the standard pattern (RB chapter.verse).

7. Joan Chittister, *Wisdom Distilled from the Daily: Living the Rule of St. Benedict Today* (San Francisco: HarperSanFrancisco, 1990), 7.

8. Stephen A. Macchia, *Crafting a Rule of Life: An Invitation to a Well-Ordered Life* (Downers Grove, IL: IVP Books, 2012), 14.

Benedict composed his Rule from a wide array of sources within the Christian monastic heritage. He drew on no less than forty rules, traditions, and theological texts from the preceding two centuries in the construction of his guide. Pachomius of Egypt, Basil of Caesarea, Augustine of Hippo, and Cassian of Marseilles all figure prominently in the shape Benedict gives to his monastic vision. They also reveal his ability to connect East and West. The so-called *Rule of the Master*, however, an anonymous manifesto written by a near contemporary of great spiritual wisdom, exerted the strongest influence from among these ancient sources.[9] Even the Master, however, remains secondary to the foundational influence of scripture in the *Rule*.[10] Benedict was preeminently a man of the Word. He established his vision, first and foremost, on the pattern or way of Christ revealed in the Bible.

Benedict composed his spiritual guide primarily for monastics, but its sound principles for living and working together—as beginners in the Christian journey—have inspired and challenged men and women across multiple cultures and contexts through nearly fifteen hundred years. The Rule consists of a prologue and seventy-three chapters. I have always followed a rather conventional division of the work into four principal sections:

1. Foundations and Virtues (prologue and chapters 1–7). The prologue and first seven chapters lay out the theological foundations of monastic life and identify primary aspirations that define those committed to the Rule.
2. Prayer in Community (chapters 8–20). The next section deals with the Daily Office or the Work of God (opus Dei), the monastic pattern of liturgical prayer in community.
3. Life in Community (chapters 21–67). A third section lays out the framework for living together in community. It addresses

---

9. On the relationship between these two Rules, see RB1980, 70–73. This works also includes a detailed table of correspondence between these two documents as an appendix, pp. 478–93.

10. The definitive edition of the *Rule* lists 132 citations or allusions from the Old Testament and 168 from the New Testament. See Appendix 6: The Role and Interpretation of Scripture in the Rule of Benedict, RB1980, 467-77.

the structure, offices, and practices developed by Benedict to help members of the community stay on the monastic path.
4. Guidelines for a Consecrated Life (chapters 68–73). A final section revisits a basic theology of monastic life and its emphasis on the goal of love.

I have always found the opening and closing chapters particularly memorable and inspiring. I find myself returning to them time and time again. Benedict's pithy statements linger in my heart and soul. "Prefer nothing to the love of Christ" (RB 4.21). "Let them prefer nothing whatever to Christ" (RB 72.11). I particularly like his recommendation for the Superior: "everything should be arranged that the strong may still have something to strive toward and the weak nothing to run from" (RB 64.19). "The greatest strengths of the Rule," according to one commentator, "are its common sense and its evident love and concern for the welfare of the individuals who would embrace it as a way of life."[11] The concluding statements of chapter 72 epitomize the Benedictine way: "They are to show to one another the purest love; to God, loving fear; and to their superior, sincere and humble love. Let them prefer nothing whatever to Christ, and may he lead us all together to life everlasting" (8–12).

As someone who has sought to incorporate the Rule into my daily life for a quarter century, three Benedictine values continue to resonate deeply with me.[12] In my mind they characterize the Benedictine way. First, Benedict emphasizes the importance of *community*. His Latin phrase describes this value succinctly: *stabilitas in congregatione* (RB

11. St. Benedict, *The Rule of St. Benedict*, trans. Anthony C. Meisel and M. L. del Mastro (New York: Doubleday, 1975), 28.
12. Every Benedictine community seeks to embody those values of the Rule that resonate most closely with their own contexts. These vary greatly, as you might imagine, from one community to another, but common themes emerge among them. Abbot Jeremy Driscoll of Mount Angel Abbey in Oregon identifies the following "Seven Rich Ways," reflecting the spirituality of the community of which I am an oblate: prayer, life together, deep reading, centering on the Eucharist, hospitality, promoting arts and culture, and caring for land and environment. See the video presentation on "Life Lived Abundantly: Benedictine Wisdom from Mount Angel Abbey," https://www.youtube.com/watch?v=LuiVF2pS9Do, accessed March 10, 2023.

4.78). "Stability in the community" actually combines two cardinal tenets of this way of life in Christ. According to the editors of RB1980, this means:

> to persevere in living the cenobitic life as it is followed in that community, observing poverty, silence and humility, and joining in the daily round of prayer and work. Above all, it is perseverance in obedience, for this is the primary characteristic of the cenobite. The two elements go together: the place and the life that goes on there, and stability includes both.[13]

This definition alludes to multiple values in addition to community and stability, namely, poverty, silence, humility, prayer and work, obedience. The Benedictine way revolves around a Christ-centered community that perseveres.

Second, Benedict uses a phrase in the Rule that has perplexed scholars for centuries. The fact that this phrase is so central to his vision makes it all the more vexing. He summarizes one of the three Benedictine vows with the phrase *conversatio morum* (RB 58.17). A literal translation gets us nowhere. What is it to which professed Benedictines commit themselves by embracing this vow?[14] While widescale consensus remains somewhat out of reach, most Benedictines understand this to mean "fidelity to the monastic way of life." Certainly, Benedict's vow represents something profound and expansive. It entails commitment to a Christlike way of life that matures over time, and this is something to which any person, as well as a proper monastic or oblate, can be committed. This "way of life" includes the practice of balance, moderation, humility, and hospitality. Benedict, in other words, embraces the value of and commitment to maturing *Christlikeness*.

Third, the synthesis of prayer and work (*ora et labora*) illustrates *harmony* in the Benedictine way. I have always appreciated the holism of this spirituality. "Balance, proportion, harmony are so central, they

13. RB1980, 464–65. The term *cenobite* means a Christian monastic who lives out his or her life in the context of an intentional community, as opposed to a solitary life.

14. The editors of RB1980 identify at least three different schools of thought with regards to the meaning of this phrase. See pp. 459–63.

so underpin everything else in the Rule," claims de Waal, "that without them the whole Benedictine approach to the individual and to the community loses its keystone."[15] There is a symmetry at work here easily grasped by anyone. Human beings are a mysterious combination of body, mind, and spirit, with all three elements interdependent and integral to one another. Benedict designs a program that harmonizes life by including times of work, study, and prayer. He develops practices that enhance the interrelationship of the physical and spiritual, personal and communal, silence and speech. Instead of segregating these various elements of real life and disengaging them—separating the sacred from the profane—he offers a vision of life in which all things work together for good. He creates an environment in which harmony directed toward love and peace can flourish.

All three values—community, Christlikeness, and harmony—draw the disciple into deeper levels of love for God and neighbor. This is their primary purpose. Benedict balances everything in his way with mindfulness of the presence of God and seeing Christ in others.

The Wesleyan Way

I have always felt that Methodists are essentially Benedictines at heart whether they know it or not. Their history set their DNA long ago. The Wesleyan movement of spiritual renewal sprang out of the Church of England, which owed so much itself to the influences of that ancient monastic tradition. The fact that the prayer patterns of the *Book of Common Prayer* find their origins in the monastic offices only serves to illustrate the Benedictine footprint in worship and prayer. But you find the spirit of moderation and wide embrace there as well. The Anglican Communion has always functioned as a *via media*—a middle way—between the major branches of the Christian family.

John and Charles Wesley were Christian disciples and theologians of the eighteenth century born and raised in this Anglican tradition. They launched the Methodist movement within the Church of

---

15. de Waal, *Seeking God*, 85.

England to bring spiritual renewal to the church they loved.[16] John (1703–91), the older brother, expressed his faith primarily through sermons. Over the course of his lifetime, as an itinerant preacher like St. Francis, he preached as many as forty thousand sermons on the God of love revealed in Jesus. Charles (1707–88), one of the greatest hymnwriters of all time, blended belief and praise to create a unique lyrical theology of God's love. Many of his nearly nine thousand hymns—from "Love divine, all loves excelling" and "O for a thousand tongues to sing" to "Hark! the herald angels sing" and "Christ the Lord is risen today"—are sung across the globe today.

Both these brothers were concerned with what it means to live in Christ. They proclaimed and lived a practical theology that touched people's lives in real and life-giving ways. Whether preached or sung, the spiritual discoveries of the Wesleys and their Methodist followers did revitalize the life of the church in their own time. They rediscovered the importance of the living Word, saving faith, accountable discipleship, formative worship, and missional vocation in the world. Methodism eventually separated from the Church of England, literally over the dead bodies of John and Charles Wesley. But the community they established continued to reflect an ethos that reached back into the earliest beginnings of Christianity. Many have drawn attention to the fact that Methodism functioned in its first century like a neo-monastic community. Like Benedictine monasticism, a rule shaped its identity and common life.

In 1739 John Wesley published *The Nature, Design, and General Rules of Our United Societies*, the basic guide that governed the Religious Societies—as they were called—under his direction.

---

16. For a basic introduction to the Methodist movement, Wesleyan theology, and the founders, see Paul W. Chilcote, *Recapturing the Wesleys' Vision: An Introduction to the Faith of John and Charles Wesley* (Downers Grove, IL: IVP Academic, 2004). The best biography of John Wesley is Henry D. Rack, *Reasonable Enthusiast*, rev. ed. (London: Epworth Press, 2003). On Charles Wesley, see Gary Best, *Charles Wesley: A Biography* (Peterborough: Epworth Press, 2006). See also Richard P. Heitzenrater, *Wesley and the People Called Methodists* (Nashville: Abingdon Press, 1995) and Paul W. Chilcote, ed., *The Wesleyan Tradition: A Paradigm for Renewal* (Nashville: Abingdon Press, 2002).

A society is no other than "a company of persons having the form and seeking the power of godliness, united in order to pray together, to receive the word of exhortation, and to watch over one another in love, that they may help each other to work out their salvation."

That it may the more easily be discerned whether they are indeed working out their own salvation, each society is divided into smaller companies, called classes, according to their respective places of abode. . . .

There is only one condition previously required of those who desire admission into these societies: "a desire to flee from the wrath to come, and to be saved from their sins." But wherever this is really fixed in the soul it will be shown by its fruits.

It is therefore expected of all who continue therein that they should continue to evidence their desire of salvation,

First: By doing no harm, by avoiding evil of every kind, especially that which is most generally practiced. . . .

Secondly: By doing good; by being in every kind merciful after their power; as they have opportunity, doing good of every possible sort, and, as far as possible, to all people. . . .

Thirdly: By attending upon all the ordinances of God. These include the public worship of God, the ministry of the Word, either read or expounded, the Supper of the Lord, family and private prayer, searching the scriptures, and fasting or abstinence.

These are the General Rules of our societies, all of which we are taught of God to observe, even in the written Word which is the only rule, and the sufficient rule, both of our faith and practice. And all these we know God's Spirit writes on truly awakened hearts.[17]

Much more succinct than Benedict's Rule, the three simple measures of this document—do no harm, do good, and attend upon all the ordinances of God—functioned as a Methodist rule of life. The rule could only be lived out in community and called for mutual respect, unity, and a deepening relationship with God. The opening definition of the Methodist Society in and of itself demonstrates the importance of community in the religious life.

Initially, the classes or class meetings mentioned in the rule had an extremely practical function. John Wesley divided the community

---

17. John Wesley, *The Nature, Design, and General Rules of Our United Societies*, in *The Works of John Wesley*, ed. Rupert E. Davies, vol. 9, *The Methodist Societies: History, Nature, and Design* (Nashville: Abingdon Press, 1989), 69–73.

in Bristol into groups of about twelve members each to help pay the debt on the New Room, the first Methodist chapel. Despite its practical beginnings, however, Wesley immediately seized upon the design as an opportunity to improve pastoral care and oversight. The classes quickly became the spiritual heartbeat of the movement. Soon thereafter, smaller and more intimate bands or band meetings provided an opportunity for intense personal introspection and rigorous mutual confession. Wesley drew up rules as well for these close-knit cells of four to seven members—organized for single men, married men, married women, and single women—to enhance this intimate, confessional design. It is not too much to say that early Methodism was essentially a small group movement of empowered laypeople, like the Benedictine tradition that preceded it. For all intents and purposes, Wesley functioned as the Superior of this new community, overseeing its life and providing direction for its spiritual well-being.

Three broad themes characterize the movement of renewal under the direction of the Wesley brothers. First, John and Charles Wesley viewed life as a *via devotio*, a way of *devotion*. As a student at Oxford, the older brother pored over some of the classics of Christian devotion, written by spiritual giants like Macarius the Egyptian, Thomas à Kempis, Johann Arndt, and Jeremy Taylor. The primary insight he drew from his study was the conviction that devotion defines life in Christ and that this life finds its richest and fullest completion in God's love. Charles was drawn to the mystical doctrine of pure love and the monastic aspiration of union with God—the goal of this devout life.

On the eve of his ordination as a priest of the Church of England, John Wesley recorded the following commitment in his journal:

> I resolved to dedicate all my life to God, all my thoughts, and words, and actions; being thoroughly convinced, there was no medium; but that every part of my life (not some only) must either be a sacrifice to God, or myself, that i\s, in effect, to the devil. Can any serious person doubt of this, or find a medium between serving God and serving the devil?[18]

---

18. John Wesley, *A Plain Account of Christian Perfection*, ed. Paul W. Chilcote and Randy L. Maddox (Kansas City: Beacon Hill Press, 2015), 33.

Second, the Wesleyan movement rediscovered the centrality of *community* in the Christian life. At the very outset of the Methodist revival John Wesley described the three "rises" of his movement:

> The first rise of Methodism (so-called) was in November 1729, when four of us met together at Oxford: the second was at Savannah, in April 1736, when twenty or thirty persons met at my house: the last, was at London, on this day, when forty or fifty of us agreed to meet together every Wednesday evening, in order to a free conversation, begun and ended with singing and prayer.[19]

Intimate communities of faithful disciples of Jesus defined early Methodism. The Wesleys were absolutely committed to the importance of small groups as the primary matrix of growth in grace. Equally convinced about the centrality of community to life in Christ, Charles Wesley sang:

> Help us to help each other, Lord,
> Each other's cross to bear;
> Let all their friendly aid afford,
> And feel each other's care.
>
> Help us to build each other up,
> Our meager gifts improve,
> Increase our faith, confirm our hope,
> And perfect us in love.[20]

Third, the Wesley brothers held up the highest ideal of *perfect love* before each other and their followers as the flying goal toward which all of life strains. They believed that Jesus modeled true humanity by the way in which he offered self-sacrificing love to all. They also believed

---

19. John Wesley, *A Short History of the People Called Methodists*, in *The Works of John Wesley*, ed. Rupert E. Davies, vol. 9, *The Methodist Societies. History, Nature, and Design* (Nashville: Abingdon Press, 1989), 430.

20. John Wesley and Charles Wesley, *Hymns and Sacred Poems* (Bristol: Farley, 1742), 83. All Charles Wesley hymn texts throughout this book are cited from the website of The Center for Studies in the Wesleyan Tradition, Duke Divinity School, http://divinity.duke.edu/initiatives-centers/cswt/wesley-texts.

that the Holy Spirit enabled the fullest possible love of God and neighbor in the lives of the faithful. The goal of the Christian life, from their perspective, was Jesus's Great Commandment (love of God and neighbor) lived out through the Great Commission (make disciples of all peoples).

Charles's poetry captures a vision of this goal of Christian perfection:

> Finish then thy new creation,
> Pure and spotless let us be,
> Let us see thy great salvation,
> Perfectly restored in thee;
> Changed from glory into glory,
> Till in heaven we take our place,
> Till we cast our crowns before thee,
> Lost in wonder, love, and praise![21]

It is not difficult to see how, in this threefold emphasis on devotion, community, and perfect love the Wesleys held much in common with their Benedictine forebearers.

A Grand Convergence

One of the most obvious and profound areas of convergence between these two traditions is the centrality of a rule of life. Such a rule, in fact, stands at the very heart of both traditions. Benedict produced his Rule to cultivate the life of monastic communities with a higher level of intentionality. Likewise, John Wesley felt that his growing movement required a set of guideposts—the General Rules—to channel the spiritual discoveries of his followers in fruitful directions. This focus on a rule of life continues to be formational in my own journey of faith. But there is much more.

I have always been struck by some of the similarities between Benedict and John Wesley, in particular, in terms of their life stories,

---

21. Charles Wesley, *Hymns for Those that Seek and Those that Have Redemption in the Blood of Jesus Christ* (London: Strahan, 1747), 12.

their conceptions of the Christian life, and the nature of their movements. Seven connections stand out in my mind.

First, both experimented with solitude as a way of life that they hoped would draw them closer to God. Benedict had his cave in Subiaco and John Wesley had his curacy in Lincolnshire. Both moved from solitude to community and celebrated the way in which life together enabled them to grow and love more fully.

Second, both were convinced that the religious life demanded total dedication to God. Benedict reminds all monastics that the life of prayer requires total or sincere devotion (RB 20.2). As he entered into holy orders, John Wesley resolved to dedicate all his life to God—all his thoughts, and words, and actions.

Third, each of these men was driven by a passion for spiritual renewal in the life of the church. Benedict, disquieted by the lack of Christian influence on the secular Roman world, engaged in spiritual renewal via the path of monasticism. Wesley, disillusioned by what passed for the Christian life in his own context, helped the church rediscover its calling to make disciples.

Fourth, both were eclectics, borrowing from diverse sources in the development of their movements. Interestingly, both served as something of a bridge between Eastern and Western Christianity. They were conjunctive thinkers and practitioners who mastered the art of synthesis, both leaders embracing truth where they found it and making it their own.

Fifth, despite their breadth of reading, each of them can be described properly as a man of one book (*homo unius libri*). They helped the people of their times rediscover the Bible. Benedict drew all his most critical discoveries directly from scripture. Wesley reclaimed the importance of biblical Christianity and proclaimed a "living Word" to his people.

Sixth, religion was primarily a matter of the heart for both leaders, rooted in a transformative practical theology. Benedict spent his life developing a way of life rooted in the heart that ordinary people could embrace. Wesley took his message of "practical divinity"—God's grace and love—to the people in the fields. Both rediscovered the religion of the heart.

Seventh, both leaders cultivated communities that developed

reputations for mutual accountability. The key to Benedict's vision of monastic life was accountability to God and to other people. Wesley created small group structures within his movement so that his followers could watch over one another in love. Accountable discipleship characterized both movements.

These two great traditions represent two spiritual paths bound together by common visions, common practices, and common goals related to life together. The simple conception of "life together," I would argue, binds Benedictines and Wesleyans more than any other theme, concept, or practice.[22] Both paths declare that life in Christ immediately and necessarily entails community. John Wesley said famously that there is no such thing as a solitary Christian. In the opening chapter of the Rule, and at a time when the most honored Christians were hermits and solitaries, Benedict says that the most valiant kind of monastic is the cenobite—the monastic who lives in community with others. All the themes that follow connect in one way or another with what it means to live together. They affirm the simple fact that human beings—created in the image of God—must live in community, discover who they are in community, and grow in grace and love through life together.

The three chapters of part 1 examine the *common visions of life together*. The very first word in Benedict's Rule is *listen*. Chapter 1, then, examines the centrality of attentiveness in the two paths and how this posture in life connects us with others and opens a space in which to learn from one another. I have already made my point about the centrality of community. But the practice of community deserves particular attention because of this very reason. Chapter 2 explores this theme. In my work on the theology of the Wesley brothers—particularly the sermons of John and the hymns of Charles—I have often said that Wesleyan theology is conjunctive. As those who stand squarely in the Anglican tradition, "both/and" rather than "either/or" characterizes the orientation of their theology. But this is Benedictine, as well,

---

22. My obvious debt of gratitude to the Lutheran martyr Dietrich Bonhoeffer for this phrase and concept. See his *Life Together: A Discussion of Christian Fellowship*, trans. John W. Doberstein (New York: Harper and Row, 1954).

The Fullest Possible Love

with its emphasis on moderation and balance. Chapter 3 articulates a vision of harmony in the Christian life, a quality sorely needed in our time.

Part 2 explores the *common practices of life together* and the way in which communal action has shaped and defined both movements through the years. The next two chapters, respectively, then, explicate the two elements of the so-called Benedictine motto—*ora et labora*—pray and work. I describe prayer in chapter 4 as the bedrock upon which the community builds its structure of life. Chapter 5 on work defines that structure with reference to human dignity. The community builds this structure day by day through its actions. In the words of poet I. E. Diekenga, "And the structure as it grows, / will our inmost self disclose."[23] Sacred song (chapter 6) animates the structure of our lives. Song breathes life into the center, the circumference, into every nook and cranny. This chapter rehearses how the chanting of the Psalms and the singing of hymns reflects the infilling of God's Spirit in these traditions.

The Benedictine way and the Wesleyan way are both profoundly teleological—they are oriented toward final goals. Everything in them presses on, as it were, "toward the goal, toward the prize of the heavenly call of God in Christ Jesus" (Phil 3:14). Neither heritage encourages complacent pauses along the way, let alone stopping before pilgrims have completed their journey. Benedictines and Methodists are always "on the way," moving forward, pressing toward the goal. Regardless, their pursuit of Jesus's way reflects Jesus's own perspective, encapsulated in his words: "Take my yoke upon you, and learn from me, for I am gentle and humble in heart, and you will find rest for your souls. For my yoke is easy, and my burden is light" (Matt 11:29-30). Part 3 delineates the *common goals of life together*, then, the spiritual values of humility (chapter 7), hospitality (chapter 8), and holiness (chapter 9).

Each chapter concludes with what I have called "treasures" from the Bible, Benedict, and the Wesleys. As I have recommended, a particular form of *lectio divina* can be used with these practical resources. Given

---

23. I. E. Diekenga, "We Are Building Ev'ry Day," https://hymnary.org/text/we_are_building_every_day_in_a_good_or_e, accessed March 7, 2023.

16

the fact that both these traditions value how you live an extraordinary life in the ordinary circumstances of daily living, practices such as this one are critical. What you do shapes who you are; you express who you are through what you do. No spiritual leaders in the Christian family understood this better than Benedict and the Wesleys. The scripture passage that closes each chapter, the prayer from the Benedictine tradition, and the hymn of Charles Wesley all illustrate the theme under discussion. These additional opportunities to pray and to sing, I hope, will help induce a mindfulness in which you experience the reality of the presence of God.

Benedict's great hope was that those who pursued the Benedictine way would have hearts overflowing with the inexpressible sweetness of love. Charles Wesley's great hope was that those who embraced the Wesleyan way would be lost in wonder, love, and praise. I think everyone yearns for deep connection with God, with others, and with all creation. I believe that a Benedictine Wesleyan way provides a path to spiritual vitality and peace.

PART 1

COMMON VISIONS OF LIFE TOGETHER

Chapter 1

Attentiveness

This is my Son, the Beloved; listen to him! —Mark 9:7
Listen carefully . . . with the ear of your heart. —Benedict
Talk with us, Lord, and let us feel / The kindling in our heart. —Charles Wesley

When I taught courses on Christian history and spirituality, I loved introducing my students to Taizé in France. Brother Roger founded this monastic community dedicated to reconciliation and based its common life in large measure on Benedict's Rule. We would watch a half-hour documentary together titled "Taizé: That Little Springtime" and then discuss how it touched us.[1] In one segment of this video Brother Roger talks about the young people who flock to their community every year. He says that one of the most important gifts the monks offer them is listening. "In listening," he continues, "there is always a reciprocity. They may not be aware of it, but we are the ones who receive life listening to them. It is we who renew our spiritual energies in listening day after day." Listening—practicing attentiveness, awareness, or mindfulness—opens up life and enables it to blossom.

If you read the Gospels closely, you will notice that Jesus listens much more than he speaks. In these documents about his life, you would expect to hear his voice more frequently. Perhaps this is explained

---

1. For an introduction to this community, see Marcello Fidanzio, ed., *Brother Roger of Taizé: Essential Writings* (Maryknoll, NY: Orbis Books, 2006). Copies of the classic video documentary of Taizé may be obtained from https://www.giamusic.com/store/resource/taize-that-little-springtime-recording-vhs196, accessed March 14, 2023.

by the fact that, before he engaged others, he gave God his full attention. He was constantly listening for God's voice and sought it out in prayer and life. The God-conscious Christ of the Gospels focuses not so much on what he will say as on listening to those around him. He listens intently. But he doesn't listen with his ears only. He also listens with his heart. He remains alert to hear God's voice speaking through the people and events of his daily life. Attentiveness defines Jesus's relationships with others. His listening communicates his genuine concern, empathy, and love. All of us need to be heard and understood; all of us also need to listen, to be attentive to God, to others, and to everything happening around us in our world. When we listen in this way, we imitate Christ.

As a somewhat typical father, when my girls first began to come to me with their problems in search of solutions, I dutifully offered what I thought were the perfect answers. This hardly ever went well and was very seldom helpful to anyone. My wife, Janet, was the first to teach me about active listening.[2] She explained to me that all they really wanted was for me to listen to them. They did not need me to provide the answers. They needed to figure those out for themselves. So, after further instruction, I tried it. I actively listened to their quandaries and laments. To my utter astonishment, when these conversations came to its close, they thanked me profusely for my help. In my mind I was thinking "But I didn't do anything." Wrong. I listened. I gave them my undivided attention. Previously I was hearing what they said, but I was not listening. Now that I was really listening, our relational world changed.

The first word in The Rule of St. Benedict is *listen*. Far from offering a paternalistic command, the great spiritual guide invites us all to a reverent, ready, humble, sensitive listening. "If the rule were to be distilled into a single word," observes Judith Sutera, "it would be its

---

2. See the republication of the 1957 classic study, Carl E. Rogers and Richard E. Farson, *Active Listening* (Mansfield Centre, CT: Martino Publishing, 2015), which brings the insights of psychology and "client-centered therapy" to the world of relationships.

first word: 'Listen!'"[3] Benedict conceived listening as a lifelong process of learning. My immersion in these two traditions has convinced me that deep, attentive listening is the key to the Christian life. Listening is an act and an art; attentiveness is the complementary disposition of the soul. Abundant life—a life characterized by meaning and value and purpose—depends on attentiveness to God and to everything else around you and within you. Indeed, Benedict invites us all to listen carefully with "the ear of the heart" (RB Prol.1).

Assuming an attentive posture may be more complicated than we might think. Our ability to listen depends greatly on our capacity to focus. We are bombarded day in, day out with messages, words, and images all clamoring for our attention. Much of that noise and freneticism seems designed to silence the deepest longing of our hearts. It diverts our attention from what really matters. In my experience, one of the great treasures of the Benedictine tradition is the way it has helped me fix and maintain focus. The Wesleyan way has helped me see God in the center of life as well as on the periphery. Both traditions help us develop an awareness of God, as Brother Lawrence would say, by practicing the presence of God. "Through the centuries," observes Bishop Rueben Job, "faithful listeners have discovered ways to sharpen their listening skills. Practices and disciplines increase our desire and capacity to be faithful to what we hear and know to be the voice of God."[4] Benedict and the Wesleys discovered the importance of opening the ear of the heart to God, of being attentive to God's voice in the Word, and of listening to God in the world.

Listening with the Ear of the Heart

I'll never forget talking with my friend Father Odo Recker about the bells at Mount Angel Abbey. "They are 'the voice of God' calling to each of us," he said. "They are a perennial reminder that 'turning to God' is more important than anything else we are doing." Listening is

---

3. Judith Sutera, trans., *St. Benedict's Rule: An Inclusive Translation* (Collegeville, MN: Liturgical Press, 2021), 6–7.

4. Norman Shawchuck and Rueben P. Job, eds., *A Guide to Prayer for All Who Seek God* (Nashville: Upper Room Books, 2003), 119.

"turning to God." The toll of the bell is designed to call the attention of the world, as well as the monastery, to our need to listen. It reminds us of our need for God and for one another; it calls us home to an attitude of attentiveness to what is real. We listen to God in a variety of ways.

In his prologue to the Rule Benedict returns to the image of listening several times. The following verses, in particular, reveal the scriptural foundations of his concept of attentiveness:

> Let us then rise at long last, since the Scripture arouses us, saying: "It is now the hour for us to rise from sleep" (Rom 13:11); and having opened our eyes to the divine light, let us hear with attentive ears what the divine voice cries out to us daily, saying: "Today, if you hear God's voice, harden not your hearts" (Ps 94[95]:8). And again: "Those who have ears to hear let them hear what the Spirit says to the churches" (Rev 2:7). And what does God say? "Come, children, listen to me, I will teach you the fear of the Lord" (Ps 33[34]:12). . . . What, dearest ones, can be sweeter to us than this voice of God inviting us? See, in loving kindness, God shows us the way of life. Therefore, having our loins girt with faith and the performance of good works, let us set out on the way under the guidance of the Gospel, that we may be found worthy of seeing the one who has called us to the kingdom (cf. 1 Thess 2:12). (RB Prol.8-12, 19-21)

Benedict plays with the intersection of several biblical ideas connected with listening. First, we must wake up before we can listen. Second, listening involves opening our eyes as much as our ears. Third, the condition of our hearts directly affects our ability to listen to God. Those who are hard-hearted cannot hear God's voice. For Benedict, listening, being attentive, being alert, and showing mindfulness all connote awareness of the presence of God.

Charles Wesley brings this constellation of ideas to life in his most famous sermon, "Awake, Thou That Sleepest."[5] Based upon Ephesians 5:14—"Sleeper, awake! Rise from the dead, and Christ will shine on you"—he integrates eye and ear, seeing and hearing. Listening is so important to him that he, like the prophet Isaiah, identifies it as the

---

5. John Wesley, *The Works of John Wesley*, vol. 1, *Sermons I*, 1–33, ed. Albert C. Outler (Nashville: Abingdon Press, 1984), 142–58.

very purpose of waking (see Isa 50:4-5). He laments the fact that so many live in darkness and remain deaf to the call of God. They have not discovered real life. He prays for God to awaken them so they can reclaim their true identity as God's children. God tells them who they are, creatures who have God's image woven into their humanity—partakers of God's own divine nature. He concludes with a word of encouragement. Listen, he says, to that still small voice within (1 Kgs 19:12). Awaken in faith to the promises that are yours in Christ. Awareness of who God is and who we are comes when we awaken from spiritual slumber and open our hearts to receive God's word of liberation.

John Wesley recalled the experience of a woman who turned her attention to the voice of God. God spoke to her when she least expected to hear anything. Listening to God's voice, in this instance—in the voices of singing Methodists—changed everything in her life.

> I talked with one who, a little time before was so overwhelmed with affliction that she went out one night to put an end to it all, by throwing herself into the New River. As she went by the Foundery (it being a watch night) she heard some people singing. She stopped and went in; she listened awhile, and God spoke to her heart. She had no more desire to put an end to her life, but to die to sin and to live to God.[6]

Listening may not always entail such drama, but failure to listen may mean missing out on abundant life. To live fully, you must listen. To know yourself, you must first listen. To find your way, you must be attentive to the voice inside you and the voices around you. You take your first step to becoming who God has created you to be when you place yourself in an attentive posture and listen.

When we are attentive to God and respond in trust to God's call, the Spirit changes us from the inside out. God not only transforms our attitudes. We experience real change in our way of being and doing as

---

6. John Wesley, *The Works of John Wesley*, Volume 20, *Journal and Diaries III (1743–1754)*, ed. W. Reginald Ward and Richard P. Heitzenrater (Nashville: Abingdon Press, 1991), 194.

well. In the context of this kind of spiritual growth we need ways to maintain a continual awareness of God's presence. Immersing ourselves in God's Word provides a space in which to attend to that presence.

Lectio Divina: Listening to the Voice of Christ

We listen to God in and through God's Word. Benedict describes scripture as "the voice of God" (RB Prol.19). In his way, *lectio divina*—sacred reading—provides an opportunity every day to hear God's voice, to maintain an awareness of God's presence. "Listen attentively," he advises, "to holy reading" (RB 4.55). My study of this practice has taught me over the years that it is not so much a technique or method as it is a spiritual disposition. It entails opening the heart to the presence of God in scripture and other sacred books. Much of what I know about *lectio*, and the way in which I have practiced it, I have learned from the writings of Michael Casey.[7] As he has said, in the Benedictine tradition this practice "became more and more an internal dialogue of the heart with the text, and through the text with God."[8] According to Columba Stewart, "Although the manner of doing *lectio divina* varies, the commitment to and centrality of *lectio* is a universal marker of Benedictine life."[9]

Originally, *lectio* referred to the simple practice of pondering biblical texts that were part of the daily prayer life of the monastery. By the twelfth century, however, a more formalized pattern of fourfold engagement with the text had evolved. This new form of sacred reading involved *lectio* (reading), *meditatio* (meditation), *oratio* (prayer), and *contemplatio* (contemplation). Each of these four movements (which include a rereading of the same text in each step) offers a different entry point into scripture, focusing attention on different levels of heart-engagement. Rather than viewing this as a lockstep technique of Bible

---

7. See Michael Casey, *The Art of Sacred Reading* (Melbourne: Dove, 1995); and *Sacred Reading* (Liguori: Triumph Books, 1996); cf. "The Art of *Lectio Divina*," in *Wisdom from the Monastery: The Rule of St. Benedict for Everyday Life*, ed. Patrick Barry et al. (Collegeville, MN: Liturgical Press, 2005), 106–9.

8. Casey, "The Art of *Lectio Divina*," 106.

9. Stewart, *Prayer and Community*, 40.

study, I have always conceived this as a dynamic, relational process. It is not so much a sequential method as it is an experience of dwelling in the text and responding to it in the way you live. The form of *lectio* I have practiced more than any other is that attributed to Teresa of Avila. While reflecting a somewhat different spirituality, it resonates with the goal of awareness of the presence of God in the Benedictine way.[10]

There is no evidence that either John or Charles Wesley practiced *lectio divina* per se, but they shared Benedict's conviction that the devout follower of Christ should spend time in God's Word every day, seeking God's voice there. Charles Wesley produced several hymns to be read or sung before reading scripture. Most of them emphasize the importance of listening with a receptive heart.

> Open the scriptures now; reveal
> All which *for us* thou art:
> Talk with us, Lord, and let us feel
> The kindling in our heart.

> In thee we languish to be found;
> To catch thy words we bow;
> We listen for the quickening sound,
> Speak, Lord; we hear thee now.[11]

John Wesley, in true Anglican form, recommended that his followers read, hear, meditate upon, and inwardly digest God's Word.[12] He

---

10. See Sam Anthony Morello, *Lectio Divina and the Practice of Teresian Prayer* (Washington, DC: ICS Publications, 1994). For additional guidance on the traditional monastic practice of *lectio divina*, see Christine Valters Paintner, *Lectio Divina—The Sacred Art: Transforming Words & Images into Heart-Centered Prayer* (Woodstock, VT: SkyLight Paths, 2011); and M. Basil Pennington, *Lectio Divina: Renewing the Ancient Practice of Praying the Scriptures* (New York: Crossroad, 1998).

11. John Wesley and Charles Wesley, *Hymns and Sacred Poems* (London: Strahan, 1740), 42.

12. Eugene H. Peterson has helped contemporary disciples rediscover this organic conception of our relationship to God's Word, challenging us to read the scriptures on their own terms, as God's revelation, and to live them as we read them. See *Eat This Book: A Conversation in the Art of Spiritual Reading* (Grand Rapids: Eerdmans, 2006), 79–117, on *Lectio Divina*.

considered Spirit-led interaction with scripture to be a potent means of connection with God. In his sermon "The Means of Grace" he describes the Word as a primary place to meet and listen to God.[13]

John Wesley placed a high value on hearing God's voice through the practice of meditation on scripture. In his meticulous diary, he distinguishes carefully between times of prayer and special periods devoted to meditation on the Word. The meditation in which he engaged was most certainly the pattern prescribed by Frances de Sales in his *Introduction to the Devout Life*.[14] This Salesian way of meditation was so popular in England that it became known as Anglican meditation. Both brothers probably learned this practice from their mother. Their sister Molly left behind a record of how Susanna had instructed her in this method.

In part 2 of his introduction, de Sales describes the various phases in his method of meditation. It begins with a "preparations" phase divided into three points. The first point is the presence of God. Nothing is more important than acknowledging and abiding in God's presence. The preparatory phase also includes invocation (the invitation of the Holy Spirit to guide and direct) and imagination (the posture of open and creative engagement). After reading the selected biblical passage, the seeker adopts an imaginative dialogue of the heart with the text in a phase de Sales describes as "considerations." The third phase— "affections and resolutions"—asks two critical questions. (1) How has this text stirred my heart? and (2) What action does this text invite? The final "conclusion" phase consists of a prayer of thanksgiving for God's presence and provision. This form of meditation moves organically from contemplation to action.

Salesian meditation, with its emphasis on listening to God's voice in scripture, resonated with John Wesley's theology of the Word. He famously describes himself as "a man of one book." "Let me be *homo unius libri*. In God's presence I open, I read the book for this end, to find the way to heaven," he confessed. "I meditate thereon with all the

---

13. Wesley, *Works*, 1:376–97.

14. See Frances de Sales, *Introduction to the Devout Life* (New York: Vintage Books, 2002), esp. 47–56.

attention and earnestness of which my mind is capable."[15] What John articulates in prose, Charles expressed in lyrical form:

> O might the gracious words divine
> Subject of all my converse be,
> So would the Lord his follower join,
> And walk and talk himself with me,
> So would my heart his presence prove,
> And burn with everlasting love.[16]

What Michael Casey claims of *lectio divina* applies equally to Benedict's and the Wesleys' view of listening to God in the Word. "It is a work of a heart," he affirms, "that desires to make contact with God and, thereby, to reform our lives."[17]

Lectio Mundum: Attentiveness to God's World

A Benedictine Wesleyan way helps us listen to the voice of God with the ear of our heart. It helps us attend to God's message of love in the Word. It also helps us cultivate "a habit of listening, required to see and hear each person—and every living thing—to know better the richness, fullness, and interconnected nature of life."[18] I call this deep listening *lectio mundum*. Sister Joan maintains that Benedictine spirituality is not only about listening to scripture, the Rule, and the community, it is also about listening to the world around us.[19] God speaks to us through the world. God is just as present in God's beloved creation as in the still small voice within or in the Word. We must listen for God's voice in all these dimensions of life in which God is present and active with a message of love.

---

15. Wesley, *Works*, 1:104–6.

16. Charles Wesley, *Short Hymns on Select Passages of the Holy Scriptures*, 2 vols. (Bristol: Farley, 1762), 1:92.

17. Casey, "The Art of *Lectio Divina*," 107.

18. This is one of the values articulated by St. Vincent College on their website: https://www.stvincent.edu/meet-saint-vincent/benedictine-tradition.html, accessed March 12, 2023.

19. See Chittister, *Wisdom Distilled*, 15.

My effort to live a Benedictine Wesleyan way has never pulled me out of God's world; rather, the more I have listened to God with my heart, the more God has spun me out into the world. Our interior life and God's exterior world are inextricably bound together. God sweeps us, as it were, into an upward spiral. By listening to God in our hearts and hearing God's voice in the Word, our eyes and ears are opened to see and hear God in the world around us. In this sphere God speaks to us both in the beauty and wonder of creation and the crucible of the human family.

If you are like me, you find it easy to hear the voice of God in the glory that surrounds us. Beauty speaks love fluently. And the more we know about this universe, the more it seems to proclaim God's majesty. "The heavens are telling the glory of God, and the firmament proclaims his handiwork. Day to day pours forth speech, and night to night declares knowledge . . . their voice goes out through all the earth and their words to the end of the world (Ps 19:1-2, 4). If you have ears, listen! (Matt 13:9). God speaks to us as well through the voice of God's children in distress and across the broad range of human injustice where shalom remains a distant hope. All too often we find ourselves having to confess that we have not heard the cry of the needy. Busyness, selfishness, and apathy deafen our ears to the cry of the poor and the oppressed. We fail to understand that this is God's voice calling out to us—a clarion call to action. We must concentrate all the more diligently, therefore, "on the voice of God speaking through the communal voice of the world," claims Sister Joan, "and calling [us] to rise above the clamors of self-centeredness."[20]

We need practices that sharpen our skills in listening to the cries of the needy. I have found that the same tools we use to hear God's voice in scripture can be used to discern God's call in and through the world. In my work with Neighborhood Seminary, a movement of theological education for laity founded by Elaine Heath, I learned about how to apply the principles of *lectio divina*, for example, to the world around

---

20. Joan Chittister, *The Monastery of the Heart: Benedictine Spirituality for Contemporary Seekers* (Goldens Bridge, NY: BlueRidge, 2020), 92.

me in what is known as *lectio vicinitas* (reading your community).[21] This practice simply illustrates one dimension of *lectio mundum*. There is no better place to seek out God's voice in the world than to listen intently to your own neighborhood.

Here is how this practice works. First, plan a walk through your neighborhood and reflect on your experience using the traditional fourfold pattern:

> *Lectio*—As you walk your community, take special note of whatever or whoever you see.
> *Meditatio*—Finding a peaceful place to sit, reflect on what you saw and heard from God.
> *Oratio*—Enter into a conversation with God about what you saw and heard.
> *Contemplatio*—Write down anything you feel God was saying to you in this time. Act.

Just as in *lectio divina*, this practice of awareness translates the listening of the mind and the heart into a living response.

Listening to God with the ear of the heart enables you to be more fully aware of God's presence and voice. *Lectio divina* draws you closer to the God of love who yearns to abide with you. Mindfulness with regards to God in the world requires you to open your eyes as well as your ears. All of these practices require openness, vigilance, and patience. All these ways of listening are essential if we are to find the God of love we all seek. God has already found us, however, in our listening. God continues to speak to us, and that speech, in whatever form it takes, is always a creative and restorative word rooted in God's love. This listening, this mindfulness, this attentiveness turns listening from a use of our physical and spiritual senses into a living response to life itself. Awareness of God's presence is the foundation of the inexpressible sweetness of love.

---

21. See Luke Edwards, "*Lectio Vicinitas*: Opening Your Eyes to Seeing Your Community as God Sees It," *Fresh Expressions*, https://freshexpressions.com /2019/09/30/lectio-vicinitas-open-your-eyes-to-seeing-your-community-as-god-sees -it, accessed March 14, 2023.

* * *

A Biblical Treasure

We have been talking together in this chapter about listening, attentiveness, and the awareness of God's presence in our lives. The biblical text I recommend for your use in this first *lectio divina* experience is the earliest account of the Transfiguration (Mark 9:2-7). It concludes with words about our attentiveness as the followers of Jesus.

> Six days later, Jesus took with him Peter and James and John and led them up a high mountain apart, by themselves. And he was transfigured before them, and his clothes became dazzling bright, such as no one on earth could brighten them. And there appeared to them Elijah with Moses, who were talking with Jesus. Then Peter said to Jesus, "Rabbi, it is good for us to be here; let us set up three tents: one for you, one for Moses, and one for Elijah." He did not know what to say, for they were terrified. Then a cloud overshadowed them, and from the cloud there came a voice, "This is my Son, the Beloved; listen to him!"

A Benedictine Treasure

I also invite you to use the following prayer in whatever way you find most helpful. While written by the Jesuit John Veltri, this prayer has been used in the context of St. John's Abbey in Collegeville, Minnesota, and is most certainly in the spirit of Benedictine prayer.[22]

> Teach me to listen, O God,
>   to those nearest me—
>   my family, my friends, my co-workers.
> Help me to be aware that
>   no matter what words I hear,
>   the message is,
>   "Accept the person I am. Listen to me."

---

22. Kate E. Ritger and Michael Kwatera, eds., *Prayer in All Things: A Saint Benedict's-Saint John's Prayer Book* (Collegeville, MN: Liturgical Press, 2004), 25.

Teach me to listen, my caring God,
    to those far from me—
    the whisper of the hopeless,
    the plea of the forgotten,
    the cry of the anguished.

Teach me to listen, O God my Mother,
    to myself.
Help me to be less afraid
    to trust the voice inside—
    in the deepest part of me.

Teach me to listen, Holy Spirit,
    for your voice—
    in busyness and boredom,
    in certainty and in doubt,
    in noise and in silence.

Teach me, Lord, to listen. Amen.

A Wesleyan Treasure

Isaac Watts, the father of the English hymn, purportedly said that the following hymn of Charles Wesley was worth all the poetry he himself had ever written. It is based on the story of "wrestling Jacob" at Peniel (Gen 32:24-32). The original hymn consists of fourteen stanzas of which I reproduce three here.[23] Listen and let God "speak to your heart" as you reflect on this text.

Come, O thou Traveler unknown,
Whom still I hold, but cannot see!
My company before is gone,
And I am left alone with thee;
With thee all night I mean to stay
And wrestle till the break of day.

---

23. Wesley, *Hymns and Sacred Poems* (1742), 115–18.

Yield to me now—for I am weak
But confident in self-despair!
Speak to my heart, in blessing speak,
Be conquered by my instant prayer:
Speak, or thou never hence shalt move,
And tell me, if thy name is Love.

'Tis Love! 'tis Love! thou diedst for me,
I hear thy whisper in my heart.
The morning breaks, the shadows flee,
Pure UNIVERSAL LOVE thou art:
To me, to all, thy mercies move—
Thy nature, and thy name is Love.

Chapter 2

Community

"For where two or three are gathered in my name, I am there among them."
—Matthew 18:20
May Christ bring us all together to everlasting life. —Benedict
The gospel of Christ knows of no religion, but social religion. —John Wesley

I have a friend who was called to a ministry of healing among the gangs in New York City. He often asked gang members what drew them into this life. More often than not they said that in the gang they found a place to belong—a community that carved out a space specifically for them. They felt special. As he struggled to relate to them in meaningful ways, it struck him that the story of the earliest Christian community might provide a point of connection. He asked a group of them one day if they wanted to hear a story that he thought they would like about a gang. They trusted him enough by this time to listen. After describing the birth of the church in Jerusalem as if it were something happening today, they all asked, "Where can I find that gang? I would give everything to be part of a group like that!"

In his account of Pentecost, Luke provides a rather stunning portrait of the earliest Christian community.

They devoted themselves to the apostles' teaching and fellowship, to the breaking of bread and the prayers.

Awe came upon everyone because many wonders and signs were being done through the apostles. All who believed were together and had all things in common; they would sell their possessions and goods and distribute the proceeds to all, as any had need. Day by day,

35

as they spent much time together in the temple, they broke bread at home and ate their food with glad and generous hearts, praising God and having the goodwill of all the people. And day by day the Lord added to their number those who were being saved. (Acts 2:42-47)

Note the salient characteristics of this community. They are simple but profound. Fellowship. Meals. Prayers. Transformative experiences. Solidarity. Common life. Worship. Their life together formed them into a people who were different, with transparent qualities that others could see. Gratitude. Generosity. Praise. Self-giving love.

Luke's portrait of the earliest Christian community functioned as a justification and a template for Christian monasticism from its outset. Allusions to Acts 2 abound in almost all monastic literature. John Cassian, in particular, viewed the Jerusalem church as a prototype of all communal forms of monasticism. Little wonder that Benedict alludes to Luke's account at the close of his prologue to the Rule (Prol.50). His vision of monasticism was a renewal of early Christian *koinonia* (community). As such, it serves as a way not just for the monastic, but for all faithful disciples of Christ. All those elements of beloved community reflected in the New Testament find expression in the Rule.[1] Benedict's primary concerns revolve around a vision of a gracious community of prayer, service, and love shaped by the person and work of Christ.

The Wesleys shared this concern wholeheartedly. They attempted to recapture the spirit of "primitive Christianity," as they called it. Charles Wesley articulated their vision in a lengthy poem of that title. Here is a model, not just for some, but for all. The opening stanzas are simply a lyrical paraphrase of Acts 2:

---

1. My own community of Mount Angel Abbey in Oregon includes "life together" among "The Seven Rich Ways" of the Benedictine tradition that it seeks to emulate. "The Rule of St. Benedict outlines habits and attitudes that monks ought to cultivate toward each other with humility and charity, 'each trying to be the first to show respect for the other' (RB 72). In this, they model a way of living that can enrich the lives of all people" (see "The Rich Ways of Benedictine Life at Mount Angel," https://www.mountangelabbey.org/monastery/mai/, accessed March 27, 2023). Cf. Chittister, "Community," in *Wisdom Distilled*, 39–50.

Happy the souls who first believed,
To Jesus, and each other cleaved,
Joined by the unction from above,
In mystic fellowship of love.

Broke the commemorative bread,
And drank the Spirit of their head.
On God they cast their every care,
Wrestling with God in mighty prayer.

With grace abundantly endued,
A pure, believing multitude;
They all were of one heart and soul,
And only love inspired the whole.[2]

As an oblate of Mount Angel Abbey but living in other parts of the world across the past quarter century, I have pondered the meaning of community many times. Physical connections are important to me, as I assume they are for you. As Christians we have a profoundly incarnational understanding of life. But having said that, I can also claim the intimacy I continue to feel with the Abbey community over all this time. Not for a moment have I ever felt detached or distant. Moreover, in this post-pandemic world, I have appreciated connection with the monks in this digital world. I have been able to step into the chapel, pray, sing, praise, and reflect as part of the community across the space that separates us physically. We are learning today to think about community differently. In a Benedictine Wesleyan way, three aspects of community, ancient but ever new, are of particular significance: a fellowship of grace and love, accountable discipleship, and life together around the table.

A Fellowship of Grace and Love

The spirituality of both Benedict and the Wesleys revolves around divine grace. These traditions have taught me to define grace as the way

---

2. Charles Wesley, "Primitive Christianity," in John Wesley, *The Works of John Wesley*, vol. 11, *The Appeals to Men of Reason and Religion and Certain Related Open Letters*, ed. Gerald R. Cragg (Oxford: Clarendon Press, 1975), 90–91.

you experience God's love in your life. If we say objectively that God is love, then grace is the subjective reality of that love in our lives. Grace is relational, that aspect of God's love that establishes, maintains, and enables us to celebrate the delight of love. God envelopes us with grace—surrounds us at all times with expressions of love that woo us back into God's loving arms. If God's very essence is love, then grace is the means by which God lets us know how much we are loved. In his sermon "Free Grace," John Wesley describes grace as a free gift for all and in all.[3] Each of these elements is critical. Grace is a gift. We don't earn it. God offers it freely. God intends this gift for all people; none are excluded from God's love. Grace is an interior gift, the presence of God's active love in our hearts. Benedict describes grace as a divine power working in us (RB Prol.29–30). A Benedictine Wesleyan way seeks to establish communities in which this grace and love can flourish.

All of this sounds very ethereal, but one of the things I have grown to appreciate about both these traditions is their realism. The Wesley brothers and Benedict understood that, while wonderous, self-giving love (*agape*) is not easy for us. They are devoid of any sense that life in Christ is a simple, progressive, upward journey. Rather, it is a quest filled with ups and downs, amazing triumphs and uncategorical defeats—of deep desire to be truly loving, only to face the reality of our failures. I love the chapter titled "Living with Others" in Esther de Waal's book, *Living with Contradiction*. It speaks directly to this reality and the value of Benedict's Rule.

> It is the best guide I know in the hard work of living with other people and loving them as they need to be loved. St. Benedict never promises that loving will be easy. He is totally realistic about the demands and difficulties of any healing and fulfilling relationships. . . . He tackles the question of loving at the point at which most of us experience it, in the day to day encounter with those amongst whom we have to live.[4]

---

3. John Wesley, *The Works of John Wesley*, vol. 3, *Sermons III*, 71–114, ed. Albert C. Outler (Nashville: Abingdon Press, 1986), 342–63.

4. Esther de Waal, *Living with Contradiction: An Introduction to Benedictine Spirituality* (Harrisburg, PA: Morehouse Publishing, 1997), 57–58.

It takes a community to raise a loving disciple of Christ, and that community must exemplify the goal toward which it strives. Only a community characterized by grace and love can be "a school of the Lord's service" (RB Prol.45).

I'll never forget a wonderful conversation I had with a Benedictine monk on a visit to his abbey one day. I was interested to learn more about how he decided to enter that particular monastery. His story revealed so much to me. He visited one monastery and just loved the choral tradition there. At another, the sheer beauty of the place overwhelmed him. He found himself totally in sync with yet another community; it just felt comfortable. When he came to this abbey, he said that some of the monks just rubbed him the wrong way. That evening, in a special time devoted to discernment, he said that God spoke to him more directly than ever before. "This is where you need to be," God said. "Here you can learn how to love." And he stayed.

We learn to love in community. Life together is the key, with all its challenges and opportunities for the sharing of grace. Despite the fact that Benedict's Rule contains no chapter titled "Community," everything in this guide points to the essential need for a fellowship of grace and love. In chapter 1 he elevates cenobites ("common life" monastics)—those who have learned to live with others in community—above other kinds of monastics who lack accountability, opportunity for guidance from others, and stability.[5] Having explored the life of solitude, Benedict believed we find out who we really are in community. It may just be that John Wesley felt this even more strongly than Benedict. He claimed that the gospel of Christ knows nothing of solitary religion and went so far as to say that "'Holy solitaries' is a phrase no more consistent with the gospel than holy adulterers. The gospel of Christ knows of no religion, but social; no holiness but social holiness."[6] He and his brother, therefore, devoted their lives to creating small communities characterized by grace and love in which they could all watch over one another in love.

5. See "The Tradition of Kinds of Monks," in RB1980, 313–20.

6. John Wesley and Charles Wesley, *Hymns and Sacred Poems (1739)*, ed. Paul W. Chilcote, facsimile ed. (Madison, NJ: The Charles Wesley Society, 2007), viii.

The Wesleyan way was contagious and Methodist communities generated spontaneously. Mary Bosanquet, a young, single Methodist, established what can only be described as a neo-monastic community of women in an area of London where social needs were great. Her first order of business was to organize her little family around a simple rule of life:

1. Seek a heart simplified by love divine.
2. Expect refreshment of soul from shared life.
3. Forbear each other's mistakes or infirmities in love.
4. Beware of evil-speaking.
5. Embrace the truth.
6. Testify to the grace and hope that are within you.
7. Keep your eyes fixed on Christ.
8. Unite to advance the glory of God.[7]

For all intents and purposes, Mary functioned as the abbess of this religious community reputed for its vital piety and active social service. John Wesley frequently noted the gracious and loving nature of this community, exclaiming on one occasion, "Oh what a house of God is here for the life and power of religion!"[8]

Benedictines and Wesleyans hold one great insight in common above all others. Benedict encapsulated it in the memorable statement: "Let them prefer nothing whatever to Christ" (RB 72.11). In a Benedictine Wesleyan way, Christ holds a privileged place at the center of everything. Christ informs every dimension of this path. "The kind of liberating love that is found in those who are united with Christ," writes Demetrius Dumm, "leads inevitably to the mutual concern and support that are characteristic of a truly Christian community."[9]

---

7. Henry Moore, ed., *The Life of Mrs. Mary Fletcher* (London: J. Kershaw, 1824), 80–82.

8. John Wesley, *The Works of John Wesley*, vol. 22, *Journal and Diaries, V (1765–1775)*, ed. W. Reginald Ward and Richard P. Heitzenrater (Nashville: Abingdon Press, 1993). 70.

9. Demetrius Dumm, *Cherish Christ Above All: The Bible in the Rule of Benedict* (Mahwah, NJ: Paulist Press, 1996), 66.

Dorotheos of Gaza used the image of a wheel to portray the intimacy we experience in Christ in a fellowship of love and grace. We are like the spokes of a wheel, and the closer we come to Christ, who is the hub, the closer we come to one another. All things are drawn to Christ, revolve around him, and proceed from him. This way has taught me that life in Christ is not about judgment of others or a sense of spiritual achievement, it is about relationships rooted in unconditional love. Charles Wesley invites all into this gracious path:

> Come, let us use the grace divine,
> And all with one accord,
> In a perpetual covenant join
> Ourselves to Christ our Lord;
> Give up ourselves through Jesus' power,
> His name to glorify;
> And promise, in this sacred hour,
> For God to live and die.[10]

Accountable Discipleship

Life together requires the act of giving up ourselves, claims Wesley, and this implies accountability to others. Enter one of the most challenging aspects of community. Let's be honest. Most of us neither like nor want to be held accountable to anyone. We would just as soon be accountable only to ourselves. This signals a problem—an interior conundrum—the desire for radical autonomy in tension with our innate need for relationships in life. Community and individuality necessarily collide. Christ articulates this dilemma in the paradoxical statement: "Those who find their life will lose it, and those who lose their life for my sake will find it" (Matt 10:39). Life together requires us to navigate this paradox. Accountable discipleship helps us embrace our unique identity in the context of a community of grace and love.

As most commentators on Benedict's Rule observe, it is important to remember that "community exists for the individual and not vice versa."[11] John and Charles Wesley concur. In light of this, a Benedictine

---

10. Wesley, *Scripture Hymns* (1762), 2:36.
11. de Waal, *Living with Contradiction*, 60.

Wesleyan way is framed by three commitments. These reveal both the purpose of community and the priority of individual spiritual discovery and growth within it. First, goodness, beauty, and love flourish more fully in community than in solitude. The whole is larger than the sum of the parts. Second, trust is the key to loving and redemptive relationships. Trust (faith) in Christ leads to trust in all other dimensions of life.[12] Third, each and every person matters. God knits us together in a way that reveals the value and dignity of everyone. Whenever I have embraced and cultivated these commitments, I experience goodness, beauty and love more fully around and within me. The purpose of community—and every family for that matter—is to help us all learn how to love, and that love leads us all to our true, inner selves.

My spiritual mentor, Mark Gibbard, was fond of talking about the self in three senses. Our three selves, as we might call them, are distinct but not separate from one another. They are, in fact, mysteriously interwoven. There is, first, our present self as it actually now is. Next there is the exterior self; that part we show to the world, our public persona as it were. And finally, there is the true, inner self. This true self is in large measure undisclosed to most of us, something toward which we are moving, the perfection of God's love as it is manifest in each unique human life. The real self is a mystery. Community can be defined, therefore, as the mystery-who-is-you embracing the mystery-who-is-me enveloped in the mystery-who-is-God. Benedict and the Wesleys, I believe, conceived accountable discipleship as a discipline that enables this mystery to unfold, leading us into deeper relationships of love.

The Wesley brothers established "little churches within the church" for the purpose of accountable discipleship. The initial Methodist Societies were simply small groups that met weekly for worship, fellowship, prayer, and instruction.[13] They were laboratories in which Wesleyan practices such as self-denial, simplicity, hospitality, and generosity were discussed and nurtured. John Wesley kept these groups

---

12. See the discussion of trust in Dumm, *Cherish Christ Above All*, 71–72.

13. See the discussion of these groups in Kevin M. Watson, *The Class Meeting: Reclaiming a Forgotten (and Essential) Small Group Experience* (Wilmore, KY: Seedbed, 2014); and Kevin M. Watson and Scott T. Kisker, *The Band Meeting: Rediscovering Relational Discipleship in Transformational Community* (Franklin, TN: Seedbed, 2017).

under this close, personal scrutiny, but mutuality was the key to their success. In Benedictine communities, the leader of the community functioned in very much the same way.[14] Benedict's concept of a school for the Lord's service epitomized these very purposes and values.[15] All members of the community, though, played their part in helping one another grow into the beloved children God intended them to be. For this reason, Sister Joan uses the term "mutuality" to describe practices of accountability in Benedictine spirituality.[16]

To shift the image, we are called to tend the flame of faith with great care. Only a community can sustain this flame and engender spiritual vitality. A community of friends, a succession of care givers, a fellowship of believers helps each companion keep the flame of faith burning brightly. We need one another—we require mutual account-ability—to do this well.

> Help us to help each other, Lord,
> Each other's cross to bear;
> Let all their friendly aid afford,
> And feel each other's care.
>
> Help us to build each other up,
> Our meager gifts improve,
> Increase our faith, confirm our hope,
> And perfect us in love.[17]

Life Together Around the Table

The family that eats together stays together. The meal is a primal symbol. In the life of a community, activities involved in obtaining,

---

14. In his examination of "The Monastic Superior," Columba Stewart describes teaching, administering, and commanding as the primary roles of the superior. See *Prayer and Community*, 81–87.

15. I find Demetrius Dumm's discussion of "Discipline" extremely helpful in this regard. See *Cherish Christ Above All*, 106–19.

16. Chittister, *The Monastery of the Heart*, 43-45. Columba Stewart observes that "cenobites have the benefit of both accountability and a community in which to live it" (Stewart, *Prayer and Community*, 72).

17. Wesley, *Hymns and Sacred Poems* (1742), 83.

preparing, and enjoying food reflect all our basic human concerns: happiness and sadness, want and plenty, life and death—God. Meals establish relationships as well as sustain the life of a community. Eating together shapes everyone at the table, forms bonds of fellowship, and turns strangers into true companions (literally "those with whom we share bread") in the journey.

In his Rule, Benedict says quite a lot about meals and prescribes practices associated with food and times of eating together (see RB 35–43). "The family meal, in the monastic mindset," observes Sister Joan, "is that point of the monastic day when the love and service and self-sacrifice and Word of life that the Eucharist demonstrates in the chapel can be made real again in our personal lives."[18] One statement has always stood out to me in Benedict's discussion of these practices. Those at table "should serve each other's needs as they eat and drink so that no one need ask for anything" (RB 38.6). For Benedict, the meal elicits a servant posture and shapes the nature of the community. The theme of attentiveness resurfaces here. Meals feature prominently in the vision of the Wesleys as well. They developed special meals for the common life of the early Methodists. The love-feast, for example, modeled after the agape meal of the early church, provided an opportunity for testimony and community building.[19] It served, moreover, as an occasion for the encouragement of growth in God-centered love.

Eucharist—the most important of all meals—shapes the spirituality of a Benedictine Wesleyan way.[20] All those things we associate with meals apply directly to our experiences of Holy Communion. "Monastic life is centered on the daily celebrations of the Eucharistic liturgy," according to the leaders of my own community, "and draws

---

18. Chittister, *Wisdom Distilled*, 74.

19. See Frank Baker, *Methodism and the Love-Feast* (London: Epworth Press, 1957).

20. On Benedict's eucharistic faith and practice, see RB1980, 410–12; Dumm, *Cherish*.

Christ Above All, 133–34, and Stewart, *Prayer and Community*, 45–47. On the Wesleys' eucharistic theology, see Paul W. Chilcote, "John and Charles Wesley" in *Christian Theologies of the Sacraments: A Comparative Introduction*, ed. Justin S. Holcomb and David A. Johnson (New York: New York University Press, 2017), 272–94.

its life from it."[21] Charles Wesley described the sacrament as the "richest legacy" Christ gave to his community. "Here all thy blessings we receive," he sings. "Here all thy gifts are given."[22] Both traditions affirm that formation through eucharistic practice touches our interior life— our attitudes and deepest qualities of character. But it also shapes the way in which we live in relation to others—our exterior life. Eucharist shapes the family into a community of thanksgiving (*eucharistia*):

> Our hearts we open wide
> To make the Saviour room:
> And lo! The Lamb, the crucified,
> The sinner's friend is come!
> His presence makes the feast,
> And now our bosoms feel
> The glory not to be expressed,
> The joy unspeakable.[23]

In a Benedictine Wesleyan way, we learn what it means to be God's people, both as individuals and communities, around the Lord's Table. Four lessons stand out.

First, the Lord's Supper forms us by means of spiritual nourishment related to God's grace. Meals nourish those who are hungry. "Come to the feast, for Christ invites," Charles Wesley sings, "And promises to feed."[24] The sacrament nourishes us with spiritual food.

Second, Holy Communion helps conform us to the image of Christ. The sacrament fills those who participate with love. This meal teaches us to assume the posture of Christ and celebrate the gift of self-giving love.

Third, the Eucharist unites us with Christ in a community of joy. *The Dogmatic Constitution on the Church* (*Lumen Gentium*) provides

---

21. See "Centering on the Eucharist," in "The Rich Ways of Benedictine Life at Mount Angel," Mount Angel Abbey, https://www.mountangelabbey.org/monastery/mai/, accessed March 27, 2023.

22. John Wesley and Charles Wesley, *Hymns on the Lord's Supper* (Bristol: Farley, 1745), 31.

23. Wesley, *Hymns on the Lord's Supper*, 69.

24. Wesley, *Hymns on the Lord's Supper*, 43–44.

eloquent reflection on this particular formational quality of the sacrament: "Really partaking of the body of the Lord in the breaking of the Eucharistic bread, we are taken up into communion with Him and with one another. . . . All the members ought to be molded in the likeness of Him, until Christ be formed in them Him."[25]

Fourth, the Holy Mystery forms a missional community for witness and service in the world.[26] Our sacramental life teaches us to see the direct and intimate connection between the table and the mission of God in the world. The Lord's Supper sustains the missional community as it seeks to bear witness through word and deed to God's grace and love.

Life together opens wide the door to the inexpressible sweetness of love. Community provides companions for us in the journey who love us into becoming the beautiful children of God we are called to be. I love the image of monastics processing into the church in pairs at times of prayer. They bow at the altar and then bow to one another in veneration of Christ. Methodists often look around the church into the eyes of their companions as they recite "the grace" at the conclusion of worship. Christ binds us all together in a fellowship of grace and love.

* * *

A Biblical Treasure

This chapter opened with discussion of the Acts 2 portrait of the early church. Experience it now through the practice of *lectio divina* and open your heart to new insight through the Spirit.

> They devoted themselves to the apostles' teaching and fellowship, to the breaking of bread and the prayers.
> Awe came upon everyone because many wonders and signs were being done through the apostles. All who believed were together

---

25. Pope Paul VI, *Lumen Gentium: The Dogmatic Constitution on the Church* (New York: Pauline Books, 1965), I.7.

26. See Paul W. Chilcote, "The Integral Nature of Worship and Evangelism: Insights from the Wesleyan Tradition," *Asbury Theological Journal* 61, no. 1 (Spring 2006): 7–23.

and had all things in common; they would sell their possessions and goods and distribute the proceeds to all, as any had need. Day by day, as they spent much time together in the temple, they broke bread at home and ate their food with glad and generous hearts, praising God and having the goodwill of all the people. And day by day the Lord added to their number those who were being saved. (Acts 2:42-47)

A Benedictine Treasure

Saint Gregory the Great, the first Benedictine monk to be elected pope, reveals the sacred nature of community in this simple statement translated into a prayer.

> Link us together, O God,
> by the power of prayer,
> so that we might
> hold each other's hand
> as we walk side by side
> along a slippery path;
> and thus,
> by the bounteous disposition
> of your charity,
> help us discover that
> the harder each one leans on the other
> the more firmly we are riveted
> together in Christlike love. Amen.

A Wesleyan Treasure

The following hymn of Charles Wesley reflects the ways in which he and his brother understand the intimate connection between community and redemption.

> All praise to our redeeming Lord,
> Who joins us by his grace,
> And bids us, each to each restored,
> Together seek his face.
> He bids us build each other up;

And, gathered into one,
To our high calling's glorious hope
We hand in hand go on.

The gift which he on one bestows,
We all delight to prove,
The grace through every vessel flows
In purest streams of love.
We all partake the joy of one,
The common peace we feel,
A peace to sensual minds unknown,
A joy unspeakable.[27]

---

27. Wesley, *Redemption Hymns*, 43.

Chapter 3

Harmony

The only thing that counts is faith working through love. —*Galatians 5:6*
All things should be done with moderation. —*Benedict*
Knowledge and vital piety, / Learning and holiness combined. —*Charles Wesley*

We live in an age of polarization. Extremism threatens the stability of our world. This spirit of division not only dominates the global stage; it distorts life on the local and personal levels as well. Life feels out of sync, out of balance. External tensions translate into internal discord. It seems as though we have lost our equilibrium. In the context of this extremism and conflict, a Benedictine Wesleyan way offers a very different vision of life. It provides a pathway to balance, proportion, symmetry, moderation—harmony. I think we all long to craft a peaceful and meaningful life that translates the dissonance of our time into a song of hope and praise. We yearn for balance and harmony in our lives.

I have been an avid singer all my life. I love choral music. The previous discussion of community segues almost seamlessly into this conversation about harmony, and I feel compelled at the outset to talk about choir.[1] First and foremost, remember that harmony is a gift. God loves harmony and surrounds us with it. Sheets of sound unfold in the story of creation in Genesis as God creates harmony out of cosmic chaos. God sings all that is into existence and as new voices are added to the universal choir, harmony expresses goodness, beauty, and love.

---

1. In chapter 6 I will share some ideas with you about the importance of sacred song in the Benedictine and Wesleyan traditions.

In a choir, every voice is important; all are essential. Just as Christ leads the community, the choral director draws the harmony out of the participants in the choir. The voices of men and women, boys and girls, from highest high to lowest low, combine to incarnate joyful sounds. Moreover, the harmony of the choir affects the larger community out of which it is drawn. The world of harmony gives us joy and enables us to enter into the inexpressible sweetness of love.

The Shona of Zimbabwe have a lovely saying: "If you can talk, you can sing; if you can walk, you can dance." God invites us to sing together—to share in the harmony of the universe—and to dance. A Benedictine Wesleyan way of harmony consists of a life shaped by radical moderation, a holistic spirituality, and a balanced pattern of life.

Radical Moderation

In the blog *Echoes from the Bell Tower*, Adrian Burke of St. Meinrad Archabbey writes: "Benedictine moderation protects 'the good of all concerned.'. . . Paradoxically, the key to a full life, is to understand that 'all things are to be done with moderation.' (RB 48.9)."[2] Given the violence of polarization in our day, moderation feels radical. But radical literally means getting back to the root. Radical moderation returns us to a state of equilibrium; it puts us on an even keel. It restores a sense of stability and calm. The concept of moderation or "measure" pervades the Rule. Benedict seeks "to introduce nothing harsh or burdensome" (RB Prol.46). He advocates temperance in one's feelings (RB 31.17), in the use of reason (RB Prol.47), and even in the distribution of resources throughout the monastery (RB 34.1). The good monastic superior embodies this quality (RB 64.17-19) and models discernment and discretion in the community. Moderation governs the daily schedule, food, personal service, punishment, and speech. In short, "do everything with moderation" (RB 31.10).

In *Wisdom Distilled from the Daily*, Sister Joan develops the idea of "life as a medley of multiple dimensions, each of which must be

---

2. Adrian Burke, "Prayerful Moderation," *Echoes from the Bell Tower* (blog), St. Meinrad Archabbey, June 2, 2022, https://www.saintmeinrad.edu/seminary-blog/echoes-from-the-bell-tower/prayerful-moderation/, accessed April 5, 2023.

developed."[3] If undue emphasis is placed on any one element of life, something suffers or is necessarily neglected. You need moderation and balance in order to develop holistically, to live a full and abundant life. She advocates establishing a rhythm of life in which, as she says, "the natural, the spiritual, the social, the productive, the physical, and the personal" all work together harmoniously as a whole.[4] Esther de Waal insists that "balance, proportion, harmony are so central, they so underpin everything else in the Rule, that without them the whole Benedictine approach to the individual and to the community loses its keystone."[5] The same can be said for the Wesleyan approach to life in Christ and life in community.

The choir illustrates this so well. Harmony happens when the singers practice self-control and remain attentive to their fellow singers around them. Harmony includes the art of blending. You must listen closely and even fight the impulse from time to time to stand out above others. Indeed, Sister Joan sees a close connection between all these elements. "Benedictine Spirituality asks simply," she claims, "for harmony, awareness, and balance."[6] In their own time, the Wesleys described moderation using a different term. As Anglicans, they valued temperance. One of the four cardinal virtues, this disposition of the heart entails moderation in action, thought, or feeling—essentially self-restraint and self-control. As products of the Enlightenment, they also placed a high value on reason. Despite the way in which many derided them for being "enthusiasts," they sought to be "reasonable" in every aspect of the faith.[7] Interestingly, both of these strong advocates of moderation and temperance wrote eloquently about zeal.

Chapter 72 of the Rule, titled "Good Zeal," is one of Benedict's most poignant theological reflections on love. The opening verses establish a critical distinction: "Just as there is a wicked zeal of bitterness that separates from God and leads to hell, so there is a good zeal that separates from evil and leads to God and everlasting life" (RB 72.1-2). The

---

3. Chittister, *Wisdom Distilled*, 76.
4. Chittister, *Wisdom Distilled*, 77.
5. de Waal, *Seeking God*, 85.
6. Chittister, *Wisdom Distilled*, 70.
7. See Rack, *Reasonable Enthusiast*.

chapter actually demonstrates the importance of balance and modera-tion.[8] What distinguishes good zeal from its counterpart is the practice of fervent love in all you do. John Wesley's sermon "On Zeal" focuses on the misunderstood impulse of "religious zeal."[9] He proceeds to demonstrate how true zeal—"the queen of all graces (III.12)"—is actu-ally an expression of deep and abiding love. The "properties of love," as he calls them, that characterize true zeal, include humility, meek-ness, and patience, all of which moderate the soul and reveal the rule of God's love in the heart. Wesley concludes his sermon with a plea to hold works of piety and works of mercy together, just one illustration of the balanced or holistic spirituality that Benedictines and Wesleyans hold in common.

A Holistic Spirituality

Both Benedict and the Wesleys synthesize elements of Christian theology and practice that other Christians frequently separate. In my experience, in fact, most people prefer to draw clear lines of distinc-tion between action versus contemplation, personal salvation versus social action, tradition versus innovation, the physical versus the spiri-tual, the sacred versus the secular, individual rights versus communal responsibilities. They dissolve these tensions—destroy the harmony—by opting for one element at the expense of the other. They exchange the "and" for a "versus" and tear apart those things that are meant to be together. But this is not the Benedictine Wesleyan way. This way holds opposites together, embraces the tensions, and celebrates the peace and harmony that blending creates. Sister Joan puts the issue rather bluntly by means of an admonition: "Be sure that one part of your life is not warring against the other."[10]

The holism of this alternative path can be viewed from several dif-ferent angles. First, this way conceives the human person holistically as a unity of body, mind, and soul. Second, it understands redemption

8. See the excellent discussion of this chapter of Benedict's Rule in Chittister, "Good Zeal," *The Monastery of the Heart*, 123–25.
9. See Wesley, *Works*, 3:308–21.
10. Chittister, *Wisdom Distilled*, 78.

as a process that harmonizes the need for forgiveness with the hope of restoration. Third, this way advocates a balanced life in which head and heart, and prayer and work, are fully integrated in the practice of the faith.

Personal harmony. In her chapter on "Balance" in *Seeking God,* Esther de Waal writes: "St. Benedict insisted that since body, mind, and spirit together make up the whole person the daily pattern of life in the monastery should involve time for prayer, time for study and time for manual work."[11] I find this to be an extremely helpful way of seeing how who we are extends organically into how we use our time. Through prayer, study, and work we attend to who God has created us to be in a holistic way. This integration, including its rhythm and balance, de Waal observes, facilitates the "precious possibility of being or becoming our whole selves."[12] The Wesleys emphasized this kind of personal harmony as well with a parallel trilogy: body, soul, and spirit. In their view, this threefold nature of the human reflects the Trinitarian image in which we are created. We must find ways to give each element of our lives the attention they deserve. Charles celebrates this in song. Here are just two examples:

> He died that we might be made whole,
> Holy in body, spirit, soul,
> Might do his will like those above,
> Renewed in all the life of love.[13]

> In holy services divine
> That we might all our strength employ,
> Might body, soul, and spirit join,
> And dance before the Lord for joy.[14]

Redemptive harmony. In my writings on the Wesleys' doctrine of redemption, I maintain that their understanding of this process is both

---

11. de Waal, *Seeking God,* 86. In the discussion that follows, I am deeply indebted to the reflections of de Waal on this topic. See pp. 85–98.

12. de Waal, *Seeking God,* 93.

13. Charles Wesley, *Hymns and Sacred Poems,* 2 vols. (Bristol: Farley, 1749), 2:175.

14. Wesley, *Scripture Hymns,* 1:159.

forensic (legal) and therapeutic (healing or restoring). The forensic aspect of salvation relates to our need for forgiveness. But God also calls us toward the goal of holiness or perfect love. Salvation entails both Christ's work for us and the work of the Spirit in us. It includes both freedom from the power of sin and freedom to love, as part of this larger whole. The Wesleys inextricably connect our faith (the means to our healing) to love (the goal of God's restoration). One of Charles Wesley's hymns expresses this redemptive harmony in unmistakable terms.

> Plead we thus for faith *alone*,
> Faith which by our works is shown;
> God it is who justifies,
> Only faith the grace *applies*,
>
> Active faith that lives within,
> Conquers earth, and hell, and sin,
> Sanctifies, and makes us whole,
> Forms the Savior in the soul.
>
> Let us for this faith contend,
> Sure salvation is its end;
> Heaven already is begun,
> Everlasting life is won.
>
> Only let us persevere
> Till we see our Lord appear;
> Never from the rock remove,
> Saved by faith which works by love.[15]

Benedict's vision of salvation is very similar. In the introduction to this book I broached the language of *conversatio morum* in the Rule, one of the three professed vows of the Benedictine monastic. Regardless of the differences of opinion about the meaning of this term, no one questions the centrality of conversion in the Benedictine way. Many, in fact, simply translate *conversatio* into the English word *conversion*. I

---

15. Wesley, *Hymns and Sacred Poems* (1740), 183. Galatians 5:6 served as a critical touchstone in the Wesleys' development of this "evangelical synthesis."

would make the claim that the entire Rule and the Benedictine way of life revolve around conversion. But Benedict does not view conversion as a single act or step in a longer process of redemption; rather, conversion characterizes the whole way of life of a person turned toward God. From beginning to end, life in Christ means ongoing conversion. So, like the Wesleys, this entails both faith and love, forgiveness and restoration. Benedict's Rule expresses this so eloquently: "But as we advance in this way of life and in faith, we shall run on the way of God's commandments with expanded hearts overflowing with the inexpressible sweetness of love" (RB Prol.49).

Practical harmony. In his discussion of humility (RB 7), Benedict employs the image of a ladder. In our Judeo-Christian tradition, the ladder signifies the unity of the divine and the human. It connects heaven and earth, as in the dream of Jacob (Gen 28:10-17). This ancient symbol signifies unity and integration. Rooted in the ground (the earth, the community), the ladder provides access to God (the divine, the heavenly). Likewise, the two sides of the ladder represent the body and soul. The ladder holds the physical and the spiritual together. This sense of "holding things together" characterizes the spirituality of both Benedict and the Wesleys. We have already seen how they view the personal and social (individual and community), the Word and the world holistically. We also see this harmony clearly in their integration of the mind and the heart. I will explore another conjunction separately—prayer and work (*ora et labora*)—to illustrate the balanced pattern of life they advocated.

A Benedictine Wesleyan way embraces both mind and heart in the quest for God and a life of love. I have one brother. Earlier in life we felt divided in some ways because of our different temperaments. Phil always said I was more intellectual, whereas he put his heart in the center of everything. There may have been some truth to this. Some years later, however, I remember Phil observing that I had "become more emotional" and he had finally "discovered how to think." Some kind of crossover had taken place that brought us closer together and made us both more whole. Esther de Waal celebrates what she describes as "a disarmingly simple phrase" drawn from Benedict's directions (RB 19.7): "sing the psalms in such a way that our minds are in harmony with our voices."[16] That is simply another way of saying it is important for our hearts and our heads to be in sync. Charles Wesley decries the tendency to separate these areas of the Christian life and, in one stanza of a hymn, provides three different ways to conceive the harmony of head and heart:

> Unite the pair so long disjoined
> Knowledge and vital piety,
> Learning and holiness combined,
> And truth and love let people see.[17]

When head and heart are properly balanced, our hands get involved as well.

A Balanced Pattern of Life

The Benedictine motto, *ora et labor*, reflects not only twin emphases within the tradition but a balanced pattern of life. Indeed, monastics have been concerned about prayer and work and the relationship between them since the earliest days of the movement. The same could be said about the Wesleyan tradition that sought to harmonize work and prayer.[18] The relationship between prayer and work is often seen as a matter of preference in terms of personal spirituality—following either a contemplative path or one focused on action. But in a Benedictine Wesleyan approach to this issue, both practices are important and the interrelationship is much more dynamic.

In his chapter on daily manual labor in the Rule, Benedict seamlessly harmonizes work and mindfulness (prayer) to establish a rhythm of life: "Idleness is the enemy of the soul. Therefore, the community members should have specified times for manual labor and for sacred reading" (RB 48.1). In his view, both practices are required in the

16. de Waal, *Seeking God*, 89.

17. Charles Wesley, *Hymns for Children* (Bristol: Farley, 1763), 35–36.

18. See Geoffrey Wainwright, "*Ora et Labora*: Benedictines and Wesleyans at Prayer and at Work," in *Saint Brigid of Kildare: Methodist—Benedictine Consultation*, Occasional Papers #2, ed. Michael G. Cartwright (Nashville: Upper Room, 2006), 9–22.

recovery of the image of God. One of the most prominent features of the Rule is the lengthy section dealing with the life of prayer in community (RB 8-19). Described as the *opus Dei* or the work of God (more on this in the next chapter), Benedict's directions establish a regularized pattern of prayer integrated with work in the life of the community. While Benedict may have had no direct contact with his contemporary, Isidore of Seville, this bishop's statement about prayer and work demonstrates that they must have been kindred spirits. "To pray without working is to lift up one's heart without lifting up one's hands," claims Isidore, "to work without praying is to lift up one's hands without lifting up one's heart; therefore it is necessary both to pray and to work."[19]

The Wesleys maintained the integral nature of the heart and the hands as well. We get some clues about this from Charles's interpretation of the story of Jesus, Mary, and Martha in Luke 10.

> Now as they went on their way, he entered a certain village where a woman named Martha welcomed him. She had a sister named Mary, who sat at Jesus's feet and listened to what he was saying. But Martha was distracted by her many tasks, so she came to him and asked, "Lord, do you not care that my sister has left me to do all the work by myself? Tell her, then, to help me." But the Lord answered her, "Martha, Martha, you are worried and distracted by many things, but few things are needed—indeed only one. Mary has chosen the better part, which will not be taken away from her." (Luke 10:38-42)

Charles believed this exchange reflected a balanced pattern of life. In every one of his references to this story in his poetry he avoids the typical elevation of Mary and the concomitant spiritualization of the text; rather, he applauds both hands and heart and celebrates the conjunction of both in the life of the faithful disciple of Christ.

Describing the character of Hannah Butts, an early Methodist woman, he sings:

---

19. Isidore of Seville, *Sententiae*, ed. Thomas Louis Knoebel (New York: The Newman Press, 2018), III.7.18.

Walking in her house with God,
    Portioned with the better part,
She her faith by actions showed,
    Martha's hands and Mary's heart.[20]

Likewise, he claims that Mary Horton provided a pattern to believers because she "sat delighted at the Master's feet, / And listening to His word," but also "ran the way of His commands, / And ministered, with Martha's hands."[21] He points to the importance of Martha's and Mary's spirit both cohabiting the believer so that heart, head, and hands are fully conformed to the image of Christ. Prayer and work, aspired to and performed as a harmonious pattern of life, draw us closer to God and one another.

In his sermon "On Working Out Our Own Salvation," John Wesley preaches that "acts of mercy" must accompany "acts of piety."[22] Prayer provides the foundation for the latter and good works—such as acts of compassion and justice—characterize the former. The acts or works of piety include prayer, fasting, immersion in scripture, Christian fellowship, and Eucharist. Given the centrality of prayer in John Wesley's vision of life, he prepared a number of resources to build a life of prayer among his followers. His *Collection of Forms of Prayer for Every Day in the Week*, in fact, was his very first publication in 1733. With regards to works of mercy, in his sermon, he simply says: "As ye have time, do good unto all men, to their souls and to their bodies."[23] He spells this out in much greater detail in documents like *The Character of a Methodist* (to be explored more fully in chapter 5).[24] Like the rhythms of the Benedictine communities, those within Methodism reflect a pattern of life based on the biblical injunctions "pray without ceasing" (1 Thess 5:17) and "[work] night and day" (2 Thess 3:8).

---

20. Charles Wesley, MS Funeral Hymns, 37.

21. Thomas Jackson, ed., *The Journal of the Rev. Charles* Wesley, M.A., 2 vols. (London: Wesleyan Methodist Book-room, 1849), 2:414.

22. See Wesley, *Works*, 3:199–209.

23. Wesley, *Works*, 3:206.

24. See Wesley, *Works*, 9:31–46.

This is the pattern of life envisaged by both Benedict and the Wesleys.[25] The integration of prayer and work beautifully illustrates the ideal of harmony in all its dimensions. It also demonstrates the way in which love of God and love of neighbor can never be separated in the way of Christ. In my effort to emulate a Benedictine Wesleyan pattern of life, three important lessons stand out in my mind.

First, in a world that is polarized, and given the fragmented nature of our lives, we need to seek balance. Harmony is not an end in itself; rather, the integration of the various elements of our lives opens us to God's presence and grace. It enables us to experience God's fullness and restores wholeness in our own lives.

Second, balance does not mean compromise. It means holding together those aspects of the faith that often seem to be contradictory. We find strength by living in the tensions of the personal and social, sacred and secular, physical and spiritual dimensions of life. We can experience the restoration of equilibrium in the midst of polarity. We learn that all things come together in the heart of God.

Third, the way of life in Christ is an art not a science. Life is a song to be sung, a harmony to be experienced and performed as sounds and words unite in praise of God. As Charles Wesley sings, "Let us join our hearts and hands," let us "follow Christ in heart and mind," let us plead for "faith which by our works is shown." All these conjunctions represent polarities in our own time. But all the dissonance resolves as we sing the song of love together in community. In the end, all harmony celebrates the inexpressible sweetness of love.

* * *

A Biblical Treasure

Many texts from scripture advocate harmony, balance, and moderation. Note St. Paul's allusion to heart and mind in this discussion of prayer and moderation.

---

25. I will be looking with you at prayer and work, respectively, and more fully in the opening chapters of part 2 related to common practices of life together.

Rejoice in the Lord always; again I will say, Rejoice. Let your gentleness be known to everyone. The Lord is near. Do not be anxious about anything, but in everything by prayer and supplication with thanksgiving let your requests be made known to God. And the peace of God, which surpasses all understanding, will guard your hearts and your minds in Christ Jesus.

Finally, brothers and sisters, whatever is true, whatever is honorable, whatever is just, whatever is pure, whatever is pleasing, whatever is commendable, if there is any excellence and if there is anything worthy of praise, think about these things. (Phil 4:4-8)

A Benedictine Treasure

Anselm of Canterbury, the medieval Benedictine archbishop of Canterbury, expresses the wonder of "faith seeking understanding" (*fides quaerens intellectum*) in this well-known prayer.

Lord Jesus Christ;
Let me seek you by desiring you,
and let me desire you by seeking you;
let me find you by loving you,
and love you in finding you.

I confess, Lord, with thanksgiving,
that you have made me in your image,
so that I can remember you, think of you, and love you.
But that image is so worn and blotted out by faults,
and darkened by the smoke of sin,
that it cannot do that for which it was made,
unless you renew and refashion it.

Lord, I am not trying to make my way to your height,
for my understanding is in no way equal to that,
but I do desire to understand a little of your truth,
which my heart already believes and loves.

I do not seek to understand so that I can believe,
but I believe so that I may understand;
and what is more,
I believe that unless I do believe, I shall not understand. Amen.

A Wesleyan Treasure

In the following hymn, Charles Wesley piles up a number of conjunctions that inform the way we live. All of them point, however, to the harmony of head and heart.

> Error and ignorance remove,
> Our blindness both of heart and mind,
> Give us the wisdom from above,
> Spotless, and peaceable, and kind.
>
> Unite the pair so long disjoined
> Knowledge and vital piety,
> Learning and holiness combined,
> And truth and love let people see.
>
> Your wisdom in our lives be shown,
> Your name confessed and glorified,
> Your power and love diffused abroad,
> 'Till all our earth is filled with God.[26]

---

26. Wesley, *Hymns for Children*, 35–36, modernized and adapted for my purposes here.

PART 2

Common Practices
of Life Together

Chapter 4

Prayer

Pray without ceasing. —*1 Thessalonians 5:17*
Devote yourself often to prayer. —*Benedict*
Pray always; pray, and never faint, / Pray, without ceasing pray.
—*Charles Wesley*

Prayer is a vast ocean—broad, wide, and deep. We immerse ourselves and swim in it, float upon it, and bathe ourselves in it. Breathing is another metaphor that helps us think about prayer. We cannot live without it and it never ceases as long as we have breath in our bodies. Prayer is not an abstract thing; neither is the God to whom we pray. Because the God of the universe is a wonderfully complex, personal being, we can expect nothing less of prayer. It is dynamic, personal, and relational. Prayer is the mystery-who-is-God engaging the mystery-who-is-you inhabiting the mystery-that-is-community. Prayer—this unfathomable connection with God—is the bedrock practice that Benedictines and Wesleyans hold in common. The practice of prayer, more than anything else in our lives, opens a pathway for us to experience the inexpressible sweetness of love.

Given the relational nature of prayer, I want to begin with a personal question. How many great people of prayer have you known? I have encountered many followers of Christ for whom prayer was the very core of their being. But two stand out in my mind. I met Brother Mark Gibbard in Africa. My family and I were involved in mission service in Kenya when this Anglican Benedictine monk came to our seminary to conduct a spiritual retreat for our community. I will never forget that holy time. For a whole week we prayed together, studied

65

God's Word together, and grew so much closer to one another. Brother Mark was a true Christian elder and the depth of his insight came from a life devoted to prayer.

Howard Thurman is another witness that comes immediately to mind. I first met this radiant African American Quaker when I was a seminary student at Duke Divinity School. The times I remember most vividly were informal conversations that he and I shared on the periphery of main events. Whenever he talked about God, his eyes sparkled and danced. It was as though he had been filled with positive, life-giving energy and his joy and total engagement with life was contagious. "In life there is nothing more important than prayer," he admonished me. "God has created us in such a way that everything we do flows from our center—our heart. Make sure that your heart belongs to God."

All of us are novices in prayer if we are honest with ourselves. Brother Mark and Howard Thurman would have been the first to acknowledge this about themselves. We all need instruction. Benedict and the Wesleys offer guidance for a life of prayer that carries us more fully into the heart of God and out into the world that God loves. Sister Joan, in her discussion of prayer in *Wisdom Distilled from the Daily*, identifies several characteristics of prayer in the Benedictine tradition. It is regular, universal, converting, reflective, and communal.[1] Benedictine spirituality revolves around a shared interest in cultivating an awareness of the presence of God in all things. In his book *Prayer and Devotional Life of United Methodists*, Steve Harper explores some of the salient themes in Wesleyan spirituality.[2] *Lectio divina* and prayer constitute the primary disciplines of spiritual formation in the Wesleyan tradition. Harper conceives the cultivation of prayer as a journey, not an attainment, and describes the essence of prayer as communion (heart) and compassion (life). Conversion of life and communion with God stand at the heart of both traditions.

---

1. See Chittister, *Wisdom Distilled*, 29–30. I am indebted also in this regard to Korneel Vermeiren, *Praying with Benedict: Prayer in the Rule of St. Benedict*, trans. Richard Yeo (Spencer, MA: Cistercian Publications, 1999); and Michael Casey, "St. Benedict's Approach to Prayer," *Cistercian Studies* 15 (1980): 327–43.

2. Steve Harper, *Prayer and Devotional Life of United Methodists* (Nashville: Abingdon Press, 1999).

In my primer on prayer titled *Changed from Glory into Glory* I explore Wesleyan prayer and its transformative goal.[3] Attentive, responsive, unceasing, corporate, and eucharistic prayer are means of grace that help create and sustain intimacy with God and reveal to us our true selves. Irenaeus, one of the great saints of the early church, once observed that nothing brings greater glory to God than the human being fully alive. Each of our lives is meant to be an act of praise to God's glory. Prayer provides the key to glorifying God. In the life of prayer, it is always important to remember that "the God of all grace, who has called you to his eternal glory in Christ, will himself restore, support, strengthen, and establish you" (1 Pet 5:10). A Benedictine Wesleyan way invites you into a transformative journey nurtured by corporate prayer, personal prayer, and silence, all of which help cultivate a deep mindfulness of God's presence.

The Divine Office—Corporate Prayer

Benedict and the Wesleys grounded their way of prayer on Jesus's own practice. Constancy in prayer characterized his life from beginning to end, his parable about a persistent widow reinforcing this image. Luke tells us the story's meaning up front: "Then Jesus told them a parable about their need to pray always and not to lose heart" (Luke 18:1). The scriptures upon which Jesus had been raised, and particularly the Psalms, stressed this prayer without ceasing. Psalm 119 might be titled "The Psalm of Ceaseless Prayer." The psalmist meditates "all day long" (v. 97). "Seven times a day I praise you for your righteous ordinances" (v. 164). This verse, in fact, provided the impetus for Benedict's pattern of corporate prayer in the monastery, what he called the Divine Office or *opus Dei* (Work of God). The Wesleys emulated Paul's injunction to "pray without ceasing" (1 Thess 5:17) by beginning and ending every day with Morning and Evening, but remaining in a spirit of prayer in the in-between time.

When I first read Benedict's Rule, I confess my disappointment at finding so little about prayer per se. Having considered him to be a

---

3. See Paul W. Chilcote, *Changed from Glory into Glory: Wesleyan Prayer for Transformation* (Nashville: Upper Room Books, 2005).

spiritual master I expected to find something constituting a "theology of prayer" in his writings. But he seemed to be more intent on laying out the pattern or establishing an orderly system of prayer for the community. Regardless, there are several windows into prayer in the Rule that provide insight beyond the structure of prayer he established. In chapter 20 Benedict discusses "reverence at prayer." His reflections on the observance of Lent (chapter 49) provide an opportunity to describe "tearful prayer" and "compunction of heart," both related directly to aspects of personal prayer. He introduces the importance of silence in chapters 42 and 52. But the Divine Office is the heart of the monastic community's life, a fact that led Benedict to proclaim: "Indeed, let nothing be preferred to the Work of God [opus Dei]" (RB 43.3). I will never forget when Father Odo at Mount Angel Abbey told me that whenever they hear the ringing of the bell for prayers, they immediately drop whatever they are doing. "Even if I am in mid-sentence, in the middle of writing a letter," he said, "I put down my pen and make my way to the chapel (the prescription of RB 43.1-2). This made a deep and lasting impression on me.

Benedict devotes twelve chapters of the Rule to the organization of the Divine Office (RB 8-19).[4] He develops a meticulous schedule for the community to gather for prayer eight times a day in the oratory.[5] The Hours, as they are also called, begin soon after midnight with Vigils, are followed at daybreak with Lauds, and continue sequentially through the course of the day, concluding with Compline as the final community event of the evening. Everything else in the life of the community revolves around this schedule of communal prayer. Benedict developed these communal acts of prayer almost exclusively around the Psalms

---

4. On the history and meaning of the Divine Office, or Liturgy of the Hours, see Robert Taft, *The Liturgy of the Hours in East and West: The Origins of the Divine Office and Its Meaning for Today*, 2nd rev. ed. (Collegeville, MN: Liturgical Press, 1993).

5. Essentially, Benedict's prescribed pattern of prayer included one night Office (Vigils or Matins) and seven daily Offices: Lauds (daybreak), Prime (6:00 a.m.), Terce (9:00 am), Sext (12:00 noon), None (3:00 p.m.), Vespers (6:00 p.m.), and Compline (before retiring).

and the Bible.[6] Even many of the prayers that are recited together daily, like the Lord's Prayer and the Magnificat, are drawn from scripture. The Divine Office immerses the community daily and repeatedly in these sacred texts, as Demetrius Dumm explains, to immerse the community "in a world where God's presence is felt and where God's goodness is praised."[7] Benedict offered this way of prayer as a means of praying without ceasing in community.

The Wesleys inherited this established pattern of prayer in the abbreviated form developed by the Protestant reformers of the sixteenth century. Cognizant of the fact that the common person would never be able to devote this kind of time to prayer throughout the course of the day, in England Thomas Cranmer conflated and simplified the Offices into two—one to begin the day and one to end it. He included Morning and Evening Prayer, therefore, in the Anglican *Book of Common Prayer*.[8] As dutiful priests of the Church of England, both John and Charles Wesley prayed these forms of prayer every day of their life. Every morning began with the words of Psalm 51, or some other scriptural sentence: "The sacrifices of God are a broken spirit; a broken and contrite heart, O God, you will not despise" (v. 17 ESV).

They confessed their sin and heard the words of absolution. They recited the Lord's Prayer. They proclaimed the majesty and praise of God through biblical and ancient forms of prayer, particularly the systematic recitation of the Psalter. They engaged in *lectio continua*, a continual reading of scripture. They recited the Apostles' Creed. They

---

6. Columba Stewart claims that "the many forms of monastic prayer, communal and private, all centre on the biblical Word. The Bible was the source and context of early monastic prayer" (*Prayer and Community*, 31). With regard to the central place of the Psalms in Benedictine monastic life, see Frank J. Matera, *Praying the Psalms in the Voice of Christ: A Christological Reading of the Psalms in the Liturgy of the Hours* (Collegeville, MN: Liturgical Press, 2023). Benedict originally prescribed a weekly recitation of the entire Psalter (RB 18). I will be discussing the Psalms more fully under the rubric of sacred song in chapter 6.

7. Demetrius Dumm, "The Work of God," in Barry, *Wisdom from the Monastery*, 104.

8. For an examination of the Anglican revision of monastic prayer forms, see Zac Hicks, *Worship by Faith Alone: Thomas Cranmer, The Book of Common Prayer, and the Reformation of Liturgy* (Downers Grove, IL: IVP Academic, 2023).

received the words of this blessing: "The grace of our Lord Jesus Christ, and the love of God, and the fellowship of the Holy Ghost, be with you all evermore. Amen." They ended every day with Evening Prayer and its similar pattern that reminded them who they were and to whom they belonged. Over the course of their lives, they prayed the following words, perhaps as many as 150,000 times. "Glory be to the Father, and to the Son, and to the Holy Ghost; As it was in the beginning, is now, and ever shall be, world without end. Amen." Can you imagine the shaping influence of this habituated form of prayer? Echoes from these prayers can be heard throughout John's sermons and the hymns of brother Charles.

Formal times of community prayer in a Benedictine Wesleyan way are not designed to take you out of the world to find God; rather, they are a reminder of God's presence in every aspect of life. From my own experience of this way of prayer, I would say that communal, liturgical prayer draws us out of ourselves in order to form within us a larger vision of life. I must confess that when I first started to frame my day with the recitation of Morning and Evening Prayer, I found it to be a boring intrusion in my life. It took a lot of willpower to stay with it. But little by little I began to learn. Increasingly I appreciated the regularity. I enjoyed the moments of reflection. The prayers became transforming, re-forming. Most important, I think, habituated prayer has the power to cultivate a consciousness of God in the midst of life. And that is why Benedict says, "We believe that the divine presence is everywhere. . . . We should believe this to be especially true when we take part in the Divine Office" (RB 19.1-2).

Disciplined corporate prayer shapes character. Denis Hubert concludes that "the monastic 'way' is a liturgical way, a way that leads us through celebrating of the mystery of Christ towards personal and communal incorporation into it."[9] The Wesleys believed that praying with others shapes the Savior in the soul. Habituated practices make us who we are. In the end, because of the support we receive from others in a life of prayer in community, our prayer becomes our breath and

9. Denis Hubert, "The Divine Office, Heart of a Monastic Community's Life," in *Saint Benedict of Nursia*, 17.

our breath becomes our prayer. We live into what it means to pray with constancy and sing with Charles Wesley:

> Pray, without ceasing pray,
> (Your Captain gives the word)
> His summons cheerfully obey,
> And call upon the Lord;
> To God your every want
> In instant prayer display,
> Pray always; pray, and never faint,
> Pray, without ceasing pray.
>
> Pour out your souls to God,
> And bow them with your knees,
> And spread your hearts and hands abroad,
> And pray for Zion's peace;
> Your fellow pilgrims bear
> Forever on your mind;
> Extend the arms of mighty prayer,
> Ingrasping humankind.[10]

A Matter of the Heart—Personal Prayer

In a Benedictine Wesleyan way, we move seamlessly from corporate to personal prayer. "Common prayer is nurtured and deepened by private prayer," observes Columba Stewart, "just as private prayer is energized by corporate experience of the Word in the liturgy."[11] Benedict leaves ample time for individuals to engage in private prayer alongside the Divine Office. To each person under his care, he says, "devote yourself often to prayer" (RB 4.56), meaning deep, personal prayer. For John Wesley, nothing was more important than this foundational practice. In his sermon "The Wilderness States," reflecting on the difficulties that many experience in the life of prayer, he observes:

---

10. Wesley, *Hymns and Sacred Poems* (1749), 1:238–39.
11. Stewart, *Prayer and Community*, 32.

Perhaps no sin of omission more frequently occasions deadness of spirit than the neglect of private prayer. The lack of prayer cannot be supplied by any other ordinance whatever. Nothing can be more plain than that the life of God in the soul does not continue, much less increase, unless we use all opportunities of communing with God and pouring out our hearts before God.[12]

Both Benedict and the Wesleys embrace a spirituality of the heart in which personal prayer plays a major role. In those elusive glimpses into the meaning of prayer in the Rule, Benedict consistently elevates the heart. He values three elements of private prayer in particular: purity of heart, compunction of heart, and intention of the heart. We find the same emphases in the Wesleys.

Purity of heart. Benedict refers to purity no less than three times in a brief chapter on reverence at prayer (RB 20), signaling its importance. We approach God with "purity of devotion" (RB 20.2) and pray "in purity of heart" (RB 20.3). Prayer should be "short and pure" (RB 20.4). Michael Casey says that "pure prayer" is simply "prayer which proceeds naturally from an undivided heart, fully possessed by charity."[13] "Jesus, the crowning grace impart," Charles Wesley prays. "Bless me with purity of heart."[14] S T Kimbrough reminds us that in the Wesleyan tradition "it is through the steadfast love of God that we are granted pure hearts. It is God's love that enables and sustains purity of heart. There is no way to purity and holiness without love!"[15]

Compunction of heart. Benedict's conception of compunction is well captured, I believe, in the couplet of Charles Wesley: "I will not let my sorrow go, / Till Jesus wipes away my tears."[16] Benedict talks about

---

12. John Wesley, *The Works of John Wesley*, vol. 2, *Sermons II, 34–70*, ed. Albert C. Outler (Nashville: Abingdon Press, 1985), 209.

13. Michael Casey, *The Undivided Heart: The Western Monastic Approach to Contemplation* (Petersham: St. Bede's Press, 1994), 29; cf. Esther de Waal, *A Life-giving Way: A Commentary on the Rule of St. Benedict* (Collegeville, MN: Liturgical Press, 1995), 77.

14. Wesley, *Scripture Hymns*, 2:130.

15. S T Kimbrough Jr., *A Heart to Praise My God* (Nashville: Abingdon Press, 1996), 140.

16. Wesley, *Redemption Hymns*, 54.

"tearful prayer" (RB 49.4 and RB 52.4). Nothing grieves us more than a separation from God. Tears demonstrate both the pain of alienation and the prospect of restoration. "Puncture a human heart and it will bleed," writes Columba Stewart, "pierce it spiritually and the result is tears."[17] My father once told me that his father seldom preached without tears. This reflected his grief over the brokenness of human life and his gratitude for the dart of God's love piercing the heart and restoring the soul.

Intention of the heart. Students of Benedict's Rule translate *intentione cordis* in a number of ways: "the intention or aim of the heart," "heartfelt devotion," "fervor of heart." Patrick Barry's translation ties the tears and intention together—"tears of devotion that come from the heart."[18] Elsewhere he defines *intentione* as "the heart homing in on God."[19] The Wesleys link intention with purity in the phrase "purity of intention," drawn from Thomas à Kempis. Unquestionably, Benedict senses this same connection. Purity of intention includes having God first and foremost in our thoughts, feelings, and actions; seeking to fulfill God's will in everything; and striving toward the goal of love in life.

Prayer is "the lifting up of the heart to God," claims John Wesley. "All words of prayer without this are mere hypocrisy. Whenever therefore you attempt to pray, see that it is your one design to commune with God, to lift up your heart to God, to pour out your soul before God."[20] I call this the "*sursum corda* principle," a concept drawn from the opening dialogue of the eucharistic celebration. "Lift up your hearts," we pray. "We lift them up to the Lord." Personal prayer is this simple and this complex. It is as natural as breathing but requires discipline and deep, honest attention to your innermost self. Our hearts are not as simple as we might like to think. Personal prayer, therefore, requires what Sister Joan calls "stability of heart."[21] Lifting our heart to

---

17. Stewart, *Prayer and Community*, 49.

18. Patrick Barry et al., *Wisdom from the Monastery: The Rule of Benedict for Everyday Life* (Collegeville, MN: Liturgical Press, 2006), 74.

19. Quoted in de Waal, *A Life-giving Way*, 134.

20. Wesley, *Works*, 1:575.

21. See Chittister, "Stability of Heart," in *The Monastery of the Heart*, 99–102.

God in prayer includes a commitment to the life of the soul, faithfulness to life in community, and perseverance in our quest for love. And the journey's goal, as Sister Joan reminds us, with such a wonderful turn of phrase, is "to put on the mind of God more and more and forever more."[22]

Silence

"Monastics ought to cultivate silence at all times" (RB 42.1). No discussion of prayer—Benedictine, Wesleyan, or otherwise—would be complete without some reflection on silence. For the benefit of his community, Benedict establishes the tradition of the great silence: "on leaving Compline, no one will be permitted to speak further" (RB 42.8). Silence is serious business. He provides further instructions on prayer and silence in his discussion of the oratory: "When the Work of God is finished, all should leave in deepest silence and show reverence to God. . . . If any wish to pray privately at other times, let them simply go in and pray, not with a loud voice but with tears and fervor of heart" (RB 52.2, 4). Charles Wesley unsurprisingly links tears with silence as well. "My flesh, which cries. . . . Shall silence keep before the Lord."[23] In chapter 42 Benedict reveals how the monastic community moves from table to reading to prayer. "The whole thing is wrapped up in silence," de Waal observes, "that deep interior silence that is such a creative part of life, of any life."[24] "There are times," Benedict explains in all simplicity, "when good words should be left unsaid for the sake of silence" (RB 6.2).

I need to acknowledge that silence is difficult for many people; perhaps you are one of them. But unless we have times of silence in our lives, we will not be able to hear God or really know our innermost self. Jesus needed, and we need, silence in the course of our day as well. Benedict and the Wesleys knew that sometimes it helps to hold yourself quiet in God's presence. Silence is not a sanctuary from the noisy business of life. It is not an escape. Rather, silence is a disposition of the

---

22. Chittister, *The Monastery of the Heart*, 24.
23. Wesley, *Hymns and Sacred Poems* (1742), 240.
24. de Waal, *A Life-giving Way*, 115.

soul. It is a place of hospitality that says, "God, in this quiet moment I am wholly yours. I want to be with you. I want to listen to you. I want to receive the love you offer me in Christ." In the Benedictine Wesleyan way, stillness and simplicity create space in which you will encounter the living presence of Love.

In a Benedictine community, monastics devote hours each day to the Divine Office, prayerful meditation and study. Designated work fills the remainder of the waking hours. If you are like me, it is not possible for you to fit this regimen into your daily life. You must have realistic expectations about balancing life's responsibilities. I remember so well a young mother who came to my office one day to talk with me, on her own initiative, about her life of prayer. She had three children under the age of five. She was upset with herself because she was unable to begin her day with what she called her quiet time, and when attempting to pray at day's end, usually in bed as her only option, she often fell asleep in the middle of prayer. I told her I could not imagine a better or more beautiful image of prayer than falling asleep while talking with the One who loves you more than you can possibly imagine. The Benedictine Wesleyan way has taught me that—to borrow the words of Esther de Waal—"praying is living, working, loving, accepting, the refusal to take anything or anyone for granted but rather to try to find Christ in and through them all."[25]

Corporate prayer, personal prayer, and silence all draw us into the glory of God's presence in our lives and in the world. Prayer unites us with Christ and binds us together as his disciples. It grounds our lives in what is real and eternal, leading us to discover the meaning of life and our purpose in God's world. Sister Joan writes that "prayer is not designed to take people out of the world to find God. [It] is designed to enable people to realize that God is in the world around them."[26] In the Benedictine Wesleyan way, God, the human family, and all creation are bound together, and prayer opens each of these dimensions of life to us more fully. "The aim of prayer," Mary Forman maintains, "is that of widening one's vision such that one begins to see as God sees,

---

25. de Waal, *Seeking God*, 152.
26. Chittister, *Wisdom Distilled*, 28.

to love all that God has created as God has, to view life's situations as God does."[27]

While neither a Benedictine nor a Methodist, Dietrich Bonhoeffer claimed, in similar fashion, that the true test of prayer is whether it has led the disciples of Christ:

> into an unreal world from which they awaken with a fright when they step out into the workaday world, or whether it has led them into the real world of God from which they enter into the day's activities strengthened and purified. Has it transported them for a few short moments into a spiritual ecstasy that vanishes when everyday life returns, or has it planted the Word of God so soberly and so deeply in their heart that it holds and strengthens them all day long, leading them to active love, to obedience, to good works?

This Lutheran martyr points to the inseparability of prayer and work, life with God and life in the world. Both are necessary for the fullest possible experience of the inexpressible sweetness of love. From prayer we move seamlessly in our conversation, therefore, to the joy of good work.

* * *

A Biblical Treasure

Paul puts prayer front and center in one of the earliest documents of the New Testament. His statements continue to inspire and challenge Christians today.

> Rejoice always, pray without ceasing,
> give thanks in all circumstances,
> for this is the will of God in Christ Jesus for you. (1 Thess 5:16-18)

---

27. Mary Forman, "Prayer," in Barry, *Wisdom from the Monastery*, 110.

A Benedictine Treasure

Thomas Merton, the Trappist monk of wide repute, speaks with directness and honesty about the life of prayer. In a spirit of gratitude he prays for God's inbreaking love and light.

We give thee thanks, O God,
For great moments of joy and strength that come to us when by a strong and special movement of grace we are able to perform some act of pure and disinterested love.
For the clean fire of that love which floods the soul and cleanses the whole [person] and leaves us filled with an unexpected lightness and freedom for action.
For the moment of pure prayer which not only establishes order in the soul, but even fortifies us against physical weariness and brings us a new lease on life itself.
Glory be to thee for thy precious gift. Amen.[28]

A Wesleyan Treasure

In eight lines, the first stanza here, Charles Wesley uses the word *pray* or *prayer* no less than seven times. He leaves no confusion over the centrality of prayer in the life of the believer.

Pray, without ceasing pray,
(Your Captain gives the word)
His summons cheerfully obey,
And call upon the Lord;
To God your every want
In instant prayer display,
Pray always; pray, and never faint,
Pray, without ceasing pray.

---

28. Thomas Merton, *A Thomas Merton Reader* (New York: Harcourt, Brace & World, 1961), 343.

Pour out your souls to God,
And bow them with your knees,
     And spread your hearts and hands abroad,
And pray for Sion's peace;
Your fellow pilgrims bear
Forever on your mind;
     Extend the arms of mighty prayer,
Ingrasping humankind.[29]

---

29. Wesley, *Hymns and Sacred Poems* (1749), 1:238–39.

Chapter 5

Work

Whatever you do, work at it with all your heart,
as though you were working for the Lord and not for people.
—Colossians 3:23 (GNT)
Clothed then with faith and the performance of good works, let us set out.
—Benedict
O be not weary of well doing. —John Wesley

In writing to the Colossians, Paul establishes an important principle related to work. "Whatever you do," he says, "work at it with
all your heart, as though you were working for the Lord and not for
people" (Col 3:23 GNT). Prayer, as we have seen, entails heart work.
But everything we do in life, the Apostle implies, emanates from the
heart as well. By instructing those early Christians to put their heart
into their work, Paul simply reminds his contemporaries and us that
who we are connects intimately with what we do. Both reveal the heart.
Interestingly, in the creation narrative of Genesis 1–3, God gives Adam
work to do before sin even enters into the experience of human beings.
All of us work, and that is a good thing, not a bad thing. We work to
sustain life. Work benefits us and others. Given the fact that we are created in God's image, we have the capacity to reveal goodness, beauty,
and love in all we do—through our work, whatever it might be.[1]

---

1. Since Studs Terkel's publication of *Working* (New York: Pantheon Books) in
1972, there has been a steady flow of books related to work. I commend to you the
various perspectives of the following spiritual writers: Matthew Fox, *The Reinvention
of Work: A New Vision of Livelihood for Our Time* (San Francisco: HarperSanFrancisco,
1994); Parker Palmer, *The Active Life: Wisdom for Work, Creativity, and Caring* (San
Francisco: HarperSanFrancisco, 1991); Dorothy Soelle and Shirley Cloyes, *To Work
and To Live* (Philadelphia: Fortress Press, 1984); and Miroslav Volf, *Work in the Spirit:
Toward a Theology of Work* (Oxford: Oxford University Press, 1991).

Jesus worked. Theologians always give much attention to Christ's "divine mission"—to the "work of Christ"—so we can easily forget how Jesus labored most of his days in this world around a carpenter's bench. Common, ordinary work defined his life. The work of his own hands declares our work blessed. He moved seamlessly from hammer and saw to Shema and Psalter, from the world of work into the world of prayer. The connection between these worlds was deep for him. Prayer and work were distinct but never separate. In the previous chapter did you stop to think about the unusual expression Benedict uses for the pattern of monastic prayer—the *Work* of God? Demetrius Dumm infers that Benedict used this phrase to assert "God's prior claim on human activity."[2] The Wesleys use the term "prevenient grace" to express this "beforeness" with regards to every aspect of our lives. God is always previous and primary, the source of all we are and do. So what we do is based on who God is. Prayer alerts us to the presence of God; work unites us with God in our labor of love.

We all work. Does that feel like an understatement to you? And do we view the work we do as a labor of love? For a whole multitude of reasons our attitudes about work can be easily skewed. Before anything else, therefore, I need to make several simple observations about work in our lives. First, many people fall into two extremes in their view of work. They either minimize its value or entrap themselves in workaholism. Neither of these extremes serves us well. Second, many people feel alienated from their work. There seems to be no intrinsic connection between who they are and what they do. Work, therefore, robs them of joy. TGIF becomes their mantra in life. Third, most people value certain kinds of work over others. Perhaps the most undervalued form of work is parenting—arguably one of the most important "jobs" the vast majority of people have. Who can calculate the value of the work poured into the raising of a child? Instead of valuing certain types of work above others (the what of work), what would it mean to think about each task being done by a human being created and loved by God (the who of work)?

---

2. Demetrius Dumm, "The Work of God," in Barry, *Wisdom from the Monastery*, 103.

As we turn our attention, then, to the second element of *ora et labora* (prayer and *work*), you might immediately sense the complexity surrounding that simple word—*work*. A Benedictine Wesleyan way engages work on at least three levels. It reflects a particular spirituality of "good" work, emphasizes joyful service to others through works of mercy, and acknowledges our partnership with God in the work of co-creation.

A Spirituality of Good Work

Benedict begins his discussion of daily manual labor with this pithy statement: "Idleness is the enemy of the soul" (RB 48:1). "Never be unemployed a moment," echoes John Wesley. He admonishes his preachers: "Never be triflingly employed. Never while away time."[3] Both were concerned about how those under their care "employed" themselves. In another simple statement, Benedict places work on the same spiritual level as prayer: "Community members should have specified times for manual labor and for sacred reading" (RB 48.1). Benedict and the Wesleys conceived work as a gift, a spiritual activity. Work is not only a gift to us, it our gift to the world. A Benedictine Wesleyan way embraces what might be called a spirituality of "good" work, distinguishing those things that elevate the soul and upbuild others from those actions that corrode our humanity. In her book *Friend of the Soul*, Norvene Vest examines "three basic principles about work enfolded in the context of prayer: (1) vocation, being called to what we do; (2) stewardship, taking care of what is given; and (3) obedience, serving one another."[4]

Vocation. Benedict addresses the topic of work directly in chapter 48 of the Rule on "The Daily Manual Labor." Whereas his discussion about work relates to physical labor there, he also addresses the issue of calling. "For if they live by the work of their hands, as did also our forebearers and the apostles, then they are truly monastic" (RB 48.8).

3. John Wesley, *The Works of John Wesley*, vol. 10, *The Methodist Societies, The Minutes of Conference*, ed. Henry D. Rack (Nashville: Abingdon Press, 2011), 140.

4. Norvene Vest, *Friend of the Soul: A Benedictine Spirituality of Work* (Boston: Cowley Publications, 1997).

Whether appointed to particular tasks by a superior or actively engaged in work of one's own choosing, all our "doing" can be drawn into a deeper and larger sense of vocation in life. Sister Joan reminds us that "work in the monastic tradition is not something to be avoided. Work is not a punishment or a penance. Work is a privilege. . . . The purpose of work is to enable me to get more human."[5] Everyone should be given opportunity to contribute, therefore, to the common life (RB 48.24-25). In whatever work we do, some assignments fit our natural inclinations while others stretch our capacity and help us grow. This is one reason why work assignments rotate through the monastic community.

Since 1755, generally at the beginning of each new year, many Methodists participate in what is known as a covenant renewal service. The primary purpose of this event, which culminates in Eucharist, is to embrace anew our relationship with Christ and the work to which he calls us. The Wesleyan Covenant Prayer, a centerpiece of the service, epitomizes our baptismal vocation:

> I am no longer my own but yours.
> Put me to what you will, rank me with whom you will.
> Put me to doing, put me to suffering.
> Let me be employed for you or laid aside for you,
>   exalted for you or brought low for you.
> Let me be full, let me be empty.
> Let me have all things, let me have nothing.
> I freely and wholeheartedly yield all things to your pleasure and disposal.
> And now, glorious and blessed God, Father, Son, and Holy Spirit,
>   you are mine and I am yours.
> So be it. And the covenant now made on earth,
>   let it be ratified in heaven. Amen.[6]

This prayer invites us to receive our calling from God, to give our all to God for God's purposes, to accept the work we have been given to do with glad and generous hearts. "Whatever we do in our God-given

---

5. Chittister, *Wisdom Distilled*, 82–83.

6. *The United Methodist Hymnal* (Nashville: The United Methodist Publishing House, 1989), 607.

capacity for action can be grace-bearing," claims Laurence McTaggart, with regard to Benedict's vision of good work, "since we may do it as human beings fully restored to the full image of God."[7] In both traditions work is a gift of grace—a vocation into which we are called.

Stewardship. Toward the end of a long list of "Tools for Good Works" (RB 4), Benedict describes these as "the tools of the spiritual craft" (RB 4.75). In her commentary on this section of the Rule, Jane Tomaine identifies the motivation that stands behind them: "These tools and indeed the entire Rule are all about love: love of God, love of neighbor, and love of self. And so, it is not surprising that Benedict begins the list of tools with the Great Commandment found in the three synoptic Gospels."[8] The fundamental work of our lives consists in loving God, loving neighbor, and loving ourselves. Our work expresses these loves. Charles Wesley said as much in his lyrical paraphrase of the Great Commandment (Matt 22:40):

> The two commands are one:
> > Ah, give me Lord, to prove
> Who loves his God alone
> > He must his neighbor love,
> And what thine oracles enjoin,
> Is all summed up in love divine.[9]

Benedict believed that these tools help us live compassionate and meaningful lives. They involve a commitment to living differently from the way of the world (RB 4.20), offering love to others on every occasion (RB 4.26), and fulfilling God's commands in our actions every day (RB 4.63).

John Wesley established "The General Rules" in 1739, a set of tools for good works of his own, to govern the life of his Methodist Societies. The second of three rules—Do good—applies directly to a spirituality of good work. Wesley expected Methodists to demonstrate

---

7. Laurence McTaggart, "Work," in Barry, *Wisdom from the Monastery*, 114.

8. Jane Tomaine, ed., *The Rule of Benedict: Christian Monastic Wisdom for Daily Living* (Nashville: SkyLight Paths, 2016), 126.

9. Wesley, *Scripture Hymns*, 2:181.

their commitment to Christ: "By doing good; by being in every kind merciful after their power; as they have opportunity, doing good of every possible sort, and, as far as possible, to all men,"[10] It may be that a famous aphorism often associated with him came from this rule of life: Do all the good you can, by all the means you can, in all the ways you can, in all the places you can, at all the times you can, to all the people you can, as long as ever you can. Both Benedict and the Wesleys invite us to expand our thinking and realize that everything we do positively (or negatively) impacts our relationship with God and others. Nurturing God's good gifts—stewardship of our work—means loving the God who calls us and filling our work with love daily.

Joyful Service to Others—Works of Mercy

The third element of a Benedictine Wesleyan spirituality of good work—service—deserves separate and more extended treatment. "Community members," Benedict declares simply, "should serve one another" (RB 35.1). This sentiment pervades the Rule and also fills the hymns of Charles Wesley. While both Benedict and Charles give special place to the care of those nearest and dearest, they extend the idea of service as widely as it can be cast. So Wesley sings:

> To serve the present age,
> My calling to fulfil;
> O may it all my powers engage
> To do my Master's will![11]

In a hymn drawn from his collection of *Hymns on the Lord's Supper*, Charles indicates the all-encompassing nature of this service:

> If so low a child as I
> May to thy great glory live,
> All my actions sanctify,
> All my words and thoughts receive;
> Claim me for thy service, claim
> All I have and all I am.

---

10. Wesley, *Works*, 9:72.
11. Wesley, *Scripture Hymns*, 1:58.

Take my soul and body's powers,
    Take my memory, mind, and will,
All my goods, and all my hours,
    All I know, and all I feel,
All I think, and speak, and do;
Take my heart—and make it new.[12]

The 1780 *Collection of Hymns* includes eight selections "For Believers Working." In these hymns Wesley elevates the call to servant ministry in conformity to Christ. These hymns present at least three critical insights related to our work. First, the servant-Christ is our model. Second, imitation of Christ requires self-sacrifice. Finally, only those who "work the works of God" are truly free in life. Joy accompanies our work as we discern God's presence in those we serve:

Joyful thus my faith to show,
    I find his service my reward;
Every work I do below
    I do it to the Lord.[13]

Methodists still sing the most famous of Charles's hymns on believers working:

Forth in thy name, O Lord, I go,
    My daily labor to pursue,
Thee, only thee resolved to know
    In all I think, or speak, or do.

The task thy wisdom hath assigned
    O let me cheerfully fulfil,
In all my works thy presence find,
    And prove thine acceptable will.[14]

The early Methodist people, like their leaders, took this call to serve the present age and the plea for God to sanctify their daily labor with utmost seriousness. They believed this work was their vocation,

---

12. Wesley, *Hymns on the Lord's Supper*, 129–30.
13. Wesley, *Redemption Hymns*, 7.
14. Wesley, *Hymns and Sacred Poems* (1749), 1:246.

a gift demanding their careful stewardship. Moreover, as John Wesley preached, it was a labor of love they dare not hide:

> Love cannot be hid any more than light, and least of all when it shines forth in action, when you exercise yourselves in the labor of love, in beneficence of every kind. You may as well try to hide a city as to hide a Christian. Yes, you may as well conceal a city set upon a hill as a holy, zealous, active lover of God and neighbor.[15]

Both the Wesleys and Benedict understood the simplicity of the gospel as a way of life. They knew that to communicate this good news to others—which was their primary calling as individuals and communities—they must model their actions on the life and work of Christ. They had to act as Jesus did. Through the influence of both traditions, I have been inspired to live out life in solidarity with those people who are shut out, neglected, and thrown away. In a Benedictine Wesleyan way, we express faithful and authentic service primarily through "works of mercy."

Jesus's parable of the sheep and the goats—which is all about service alongside those in most desperate need—figures prominently in this regard. Benedict alludes to it in his admonitions about the care of the sick (RB 36.2-3). His concern for the elderly, the sick, and children (see RB 34-37) reveals his deeply compassionate heart. Referring to Jesus's parable, John Wesley observes that "the love of our neighbor naturally leads all that feel it to works of mercy. It inclines us to feed the hungry, to clothe the naked, to visit them that are sick or in prison, to be as eyes to the blind, and feet to the lame, a husband to the widow, a father to the fatherless."[16] His brother makes it clear that love must always motivate our service to the poor. Our goal is always to elevate those who suffer, not to put them down. Only love can do this work.

> Work for the weak, and sick, and poor,
> Clothing and food for them procure,
> And mindful of God's word,

---

15. Wesley, *Works*, 1:539.
16. Wesley, *Works*, 3:191.

Enjoy the blessedness to give,
Lay out your substance to relieve
    The members of your Lord.

Your labor which proceeds from love,
Jesus shall graciously approve,
    With full felicity,
With brightest crowns your loan repay,
And tell you in that joyful day,
    "Ye did it unto Me."[17]

Dorothy Day, an oblate of St. Procopius Abbey in Illinois, sought to live out the spirit of Benedict's Rule through the Catholic Worker Movement.[18] Initially, this movement sought to alleviate the suffering of those caught in the depths of the Great Depression. Day envisioned a community of God's people dedicated to works of mercy. In an article written for *Commonweal* in 1949, she demonstrated the centrality of acts of compassion and justice in the way of life she envisioned and embodied.[19] She talks about the importance of what she calls spiritual works of mercy, like counseling the doubtful and comforting the sorrowful. Equally important to her are the corporal works: feeding the hungry, giving drink to the thirsty, clothing the naked, ransoming the captive, harboring the harborless, visiting the sick, and burying the dead—essentially John Wesley's own list, drawn by both from Jesus's parable (Matt 25). Rather than obligations or duties, in her view these actions celebrate Christ.

The life of Dorothy Day reminds me very much of an early Methodist woman eulogized by Charles Wesley. He provides this lyrical portrait of love in action in an unjust world:

---

17. Charles Wesley, MS Acts, 419.

18. See Robert Coles, *Dorothy Day: A Radical Devotion* (Boston: Da Capo Press, 1987); and Jim Forest, *All Is Grace: A Biography of Dorothy Day* (Maryknoll, NY: Orbis Books, 2011).

19. See Dorothy Day, "The Scandal of the Works of Mercy," *Commonweal*, November 4, 1949, https://www.commonwealmagazine.org/scandal-works-mercy, accessed April 23, 2023.

A nursing mother to the poor,
For them she husbanded her store,
    Her life, her all, bestowed;
For them she labored day and night,
In doing good her whole delight,
    In copying after God.[20]

Day and the Wesleys discovered how acts of compassion often engage us necessarily in acts of justice.[21] While compassion represents the personal dimension of works of mercy, acts of justice engage us more fully in the reign of God. From a Benedictine Wesleyan way I have learned that the authentic self is inextricably bound to the rule of God in life. In praying the Lord's Prayer we commit ourselves to offer God's love to all and to oppose injustice wherever we find it. This vision of life challenges a common assumption of many today, namely, that morality, good works, and social justice are somehow disconnected from the cultivation of a spiritual life.

The Work of Co-creation

This leads seamlessly to the final aspect of work—our participation in God's ongoing creation and the realization of shalom in our world. Sister Joan stresses God's invitation to each of us to be co-creators. She articulates this so eloquently from her Benedictine perspective:

Why we work is the very bedrock of Benedictine spirituality. It is about the bringing of the Reign of God to earth. It is about completing the work of God in the upbuilding of the world. Work, in

---

20. Charles Wesley, *The Journal of the Rev. Charles Wesley, M.A.*, 2 vols., ed. Thomas Jackson (Kansas City: Beacon Hill Press, 1980), 2:341.

21. Dorothy Day taught one longtime associate that justice begins on our knees; that it is for you and me, here and now, right where we are; and that the most radical thing we can do is to try to find the face of Christ in others. See Jim Forest, "Dorothy Day," *U.S. Catholic: Faith in Real Life*, June 1, 1995, https://uscatholic. org/articles/199507/what-i-learned-about-justice-from-dorothy-day/, accessed April 23, 2023. For John Wesley's efforts to eradicate hunger and slavery in his own day, see Manfred Marquardt, *John Wesley's Social Ethics: Praxis and Principles*, trans. John E. Steely and W. Stephen Gunter (Nashville: Abingdon Press, 1992).

Benedictine spirituality, calls for labor—manual labor, spiritual labor, and intellectual labor—that continues the co-creation of the world. . . . We work with a vision in mind. After the person with a Benedictine soul has been there, the world ought to be a little closer to the way the Kingdom will look.[22]

As in the Benedictine tradition, the Wesleys understand this aspect of good work primarily in terms of partnering with God in the realization of God's rule. They did all in their power to create opportunities for everyone to embody the goodness, beauty, and love God intends in the world. This is what it meant to enroll in Benedict's "school of the Lord's service" and for Wesleyans to live the way of Christ in community. Whenever I have sought to align myself more intentionally with God's reign of love—following the model of Jesus—the more I have felt fully alive.

Norvene Vest invites us to discover the joy of partnering with God and making our good work count for good in this world.

Our work here on earth is "co-creative," which means it is shared with the living God. God's original intention was that work express the unique gifts and qualities of each person in the service of a unified whole, like a melody that is diminished by the absence of any single note. . . . The "work" of the reconciliation of the world to God and of the transformation of all things into their intended fullness in Christ is in part *our* work, no less than God's.[23]

Charles Wesley found co-creative opportunities within the context of his own family—one of the best places for any of us to begin. He composed a visionary hymn for his bride on their wedding day. It affords a unique window into the co-creative labor that leads to the inexpressible sweetness of love:

---

22. Chittister, *Wisdom Distilled*, 69–70, 86; cf. Chittister, "Co-Creation," in *The Monastery of the Heart*, 73–76.

23. Vest, *Friend of the Soul*, 3; cf. M. Basil Pennington, "By the Labor of Their Hands," in *Lessons from the Monastery That Touch Your Life* (Mahwah, NJ: Paulist Press, 1994), 22–26.

Come, let us arise,
And press to the skies,
The summons obey,
    My friend, my beloved, and hasten away!
The master of all
For our service doth call,
 And deigns to approve
    With smiles of acceptance our labor of love.

His burden who bear,
We alone can declare
How easy his yoke,
    While to love, and good works we each other provoke:
By word and by deed,
The bodies in need,
The souls to relieve,
    And freely as Jesus hath given to give.[24]

* * *

A Biblical Treasure

Jesus's parable provides a stunning image with regards to the actions of our lives. He implores us to find his face in the faces of our brothers and sisters in need around us daily.

> "Then the king will say to those at his right hand, 'Come, you who are blessed by my Father, inherit the kingdom prepared for you from the foundation of the world, for I was hungry and you gave me food, I was thirsty and you gave me something to drink, I was a stranger and you welcomed me, I was naked and you gave me clothing, I was sick and you took care of me, I was in prison and you visited me.' Then the righteous will answer him, "Lord, when was it that we saw you hungry and gave you food or thirsty and gave you something to drink? And when was it that we saw you a stranger and welcomed you or naked and gave you clothing? And when was it that we saw you sick or in prison and visited you?' And the king will answer

---

24. Wesley, *Hymns and Sacred Poems* (1749), 2:280–81.

them, 'Truly I tell you, just as you did it to one of the least of these brothers and sisters of mine, you did it to me.'" (Matthew 25:34-40)

A Benedictine Treasure

The Benedictine oblate Dorothy Day personified the Catholic Worker Movement. The following prayer is adapted from one of her famous statements about Jesus.

> Jesus, you are the center of everything we do.
> When I think of you,
>   I think of someone who was *constantly* passionate;
> I think of all your experiences—everything you did—
>   as part of your passion:
>   the stories you told,
>   the miracles you performed,
>   the sermons you delivered,
>   the suffering you endured,
>   the death you experienced.
> Your whole life was a Passion—
>   the energy, the love,
>   the attention you gave to so many people,
>   to friends and enemies alike.
> Loving Jesus, fill me with such passion. Amen.[25]

A Wesleyan Treasure

Charles Wesley was always concerned about the way in which our attitudes about what we do—how we live—reflect our posture and character. He titled this hymn "Before Work."

> Forth in thy name, O Lord, I go,
>   My daily labor to pursue,
> Thee, only thee resolved to know
>   In all I think, or speak, or do.

25. "Faith, Work, Prayer," *The Dorothy Day Guild*, November 13, 2013, http://dorothydayguild.org/about-her-life/faith-work-prayer/, accessed April 23, 2023.

The task thy wisdom hath assigned
        O let me cheerfully fulfil,
In all my works thy presence find,
        And prove thine acceptable will.

Thee may I set at my right hand
        Whose eyes my inmost substance see,
And labor on at thy command,
        And offer all my works to thee.[26]

---

26. Wesley, *Hymns and Sacred Poems* (1749), 1:246.

Chapter 6

Sacred Song

Let the word of Christ dwell in you richly;
teach and admonish one another in all wisdom;
and with gratitude in your hearts
sing psalms, hymns, and spiritual songs to God. —*Colossians 3:16*
Sing the psalms in such a way that
our minds are in harmony with our voices. —*Benedict*
Teach me the new, the gospel song,
let my tongue move only to thy praise. —*Charles Wesley*

Music moves us. Sacred song shapes us. Singing and spirituality are inextricably connected. When we sing together something eternal happens. Rudolf Otto developed the concept of the "numinous" to describe this apprehension, this mystery.[1] Singing has the power to arouse spiritual and religious emotions. It inspires a mysterious awe that moves us deeply. St. Augustine purportedly claimed that to sing is to pray twice, and it is not hard to understand why this is the case.

I want to open a conversation with you about the practice of sacred song using three brief vignettes. The grand Cathedral of Notre Dame in Paris caught fire on April 15, 2019. The tragedy is still incomprehensible. On that fateful day, as darkness fell and the crowds swelled in the vicinity of the cathedral, those who gathered began to sing hymns. In the midst of this great loss God's people expressed their lament and bolstered their faith in song.

I am a member of the Chamber Choir of the Bach Festival Society of Winter Park, Florida. We recently performed a concert simply titled

---

1. See Rudolf Otto, *The Idea of the Holy* (Oxford: Oxford University Press, 1923).

"Spirituals," including classics like "Deep River," about which Howard Thurman has written movingly.[2] Samuel McKelton, a member of the world-renowned American Spiritual Ensemble, sang with us and provided vivid commentary. One song in particular, a new setting of "Steal Away," captured all our hearts as we reflected on the spiritual's message of trust in God and the anticipation of actual liberation from the crucible of slavery.

I was in high school when I first heard the Concordia Choir. They had a concert at one of the major performing arts centers in Chicago. My choral director was an alumus, so he invited several of us to drive into the city with him. The repertoire included several lush pieces composed by F. Melius Christiansen, considered by most to be the pioneer of a cappella singing in America. They concluded the concert, as is their custom, with his famous arrangement of "Beautiful Savior." As a contralto soloist sang stanza two, one of the greatest honors for the singers, you could not find a dry eye in the house:

> Fair are the meadows,
> Fair are the woodlands,
> Robed in flow'rs of blooming spring;
> Jesus is fairer, Jesus is purer;
> He makes our sorr'wing spirit sing.

A Benedictine Wesleyan way celebrates the inexpressible sweetness of love found in singing the faith. This common chord (notice the spelling) that binds these two traditions together also reflects the intimate connections between music and spirituality, sacred song and life. I need to say a few things, first, about "singing the faith." From the outset I have been weaving the Benedictine and Wesleyan traditions together in each chapter, hopefully in a fairly seamless way. In this chapter, however, it feels more natural to focus, respectively, on the centrality of singing or chanting the Psalms in the monastic heritage and then the singing of hymns or sacred songs among the Methodists. These ways of singing may be different—the chant and the hymn—but

---

2. Howard Thurman, *Deep River: The Negro Spiritual Speaks Life and Death* (Richmond, IN: Friends United Press, 1975).

both point in the same direction to the God who sings all that is into existence.

Singing the Faith

"What people really believe down deep," writes hymnologist Hugh McElrath, "is often embedded in the words of the hymns they have known and loved because of repeated meaningful experiences in singing them."[3] Fundamentally, Psalms, hymns, and spiritual songs are theological speech. Scripture links speaking and singing very closely. In *The Magician's Nephew* C. S. Lewis has Aslan (his figure for Christ) sing the universe into existence through one great creative act of song. Could it be that singing is our original theological language? And if this is the case, then the Psalms and the hymns and spiritual songs we sing about our faith relocate theology in a space that fits us more comfortably than we might otherwise imagine.

As someone who deeply appreciates both singing and the life of faith, I find the insight of my friend Karen Westerfield Tucker to be extremely helpful in this regard:

> The singing of doctrine truly allows for the embodiment of belief. Because of the physical mechanisms required for singing, sung confession and praise necessarily engage the whole person: assent to God's truths is not only of the mind and lips, but is drawn from the very breath—the breath of the spirit and of the Spirit—that supports life. The breath that animates the individual body is also the breath that sustains the body of Christ, the Church, and that allows the congregation to sing with one voice.[4]

Singing involves this intimate connection between the physical and the spiritual, and this integration of ourselves helps embed whatever we are singing deeply in heart, mind, and soul. One of my mentors

---

3. Hugh T. McElrath, "The Hymnbook as a Compendium of Theology," *Review and Expositor* 87 (1990): 11.

4. Karen Westerfield Tucker, "*Lex Credendi, Lex Canendi*: Noting the Faith of the Church," in *Ecumenical Theology in Worship, Doctrine and Life*, ed. D. S. Cunningham et al. (New York: Oxford University Press, 1999), 53.

in seminary, John Westerhoff, befriended a dear member of his home church who suffered from dementia. She did not know who he was when he visited her. But if he asked her to sing a favorite hymn, she joined right in without missing a word or skipping a beat. "Our favorite songs, and those which we best remember, are the ones expressing the deepest feelings of our hearts," claims Tim Colvin. "They shout out our *feelings* about what we *believe* about God."[5] What we sing shapes us spiritually and our theology shapes what we sing.

Geoffrey Wainwright, in his single-volume systematic theology, *Doxology*, provides a helpful description of the relationship between faith and sacred song.[6] First, sacred songs have the capacity to communicate the central truths about the gospel and our life in Christ. Second, the songs of our faith help us grow in grace and live into the dominion of God's love. Jeremy Begbie goes so far as to claim that "music—in, with, and through language—is capable of enabling a fuller participation in the realities which that language mediates and in which all are caught up."[7] To put this as simply as possible, singing the faith draws us into the numinous presence of God and enables us to dwell richly in God's love. Benedict was passionate about this. He puts the Psalms—the songbook of the Hebrew people—in the very center of monastic life because he wanted his followers to experience the presence of God. Methodism was born in song. Charles Wesley helped the early Methodist people learn the faith by singing it. In singing together in this way they experienced God's deep and abiding love.

In both these traditions, clear principles governed their vision of a sung faith. First, they affirmed the centrality of singing the faith because they followed the lead of Scripture. In the Old Testament, lyrical texts like the Song of Miriam (Exod 15:20-21) reminded the people of Israel that they served a God who acts in human history. In

5. Thomas S. Colvin, "Global Song and Theology: Content," in *Music & Mission*, edited by S T Kimbrough (New York: GBGMusik, 2006), 53.

6. Geoffrey Wainwright, *Doxology: The Praise of God in Worship, Doctrine, and Life* (New York: Oxford University Press, 1980), 198–205.

7. Jeremy S. Begbie, *Music, Modernity, and God: Essays in Listening* (Oxford: Oxford University Press, 2013), 207.

the New Testament, the Magnificat—the Song of Mary (Luke 1:46-55)—inspired Jesus's followers to respond wholeheartedly, like her, to God's call. And then, of course, there are the Psalms, one of the most profound collections of sung prayer in religious history. Second, they appreciated the unifying effect of singing together. The chanting of the Psalms in Benedictine monasteries, as we shall see more fully momentarily, involved the entire community in a unifying act of praise. The English hymn, mastered by Charles Wesley, engaged the entire community as well. Singing the faith in this way transformed the lives of many. Benedictines and Wesleyans practice two different ways of singing the faith, but they share a common conviction about the need to embrace God's presence by singing the faith. Through Psalms and through hymns and spiritual songs they praise God and celebrate the inexpressible sweetness of love.

The Psalms

The same year I made my oblation, a dear friend in Austria sent me a copy of *The Music of Silence*, by David Steindl-Rast, an Austrian-born Benedictine monk. All this coincided with the release of the best-selling *Chant* CD, sung by the monks of Santo Domingo de Silos. Interest in Gregorian chant exploded almost immediately into something of a global phenomenon. For me, as an avid singer, all this enamored me all the more of this tradition I had embraced. The "music of the monastery," in fact, was one dimension of the Benedictine way that drew me in quickly and deeply. The chanting of the Psalms elevated my spirit as few things had before.

Marie-Bernard de Soos expresses well my own experience: "For Benedict, the way of the gospel is found in the Psalms."[8] Early in the prologue of the Rule, Benedict asks the most crucial questions about life to which the gospel is the answer. The Psalms inquire and speak on his behalf. "Who is the one who desires life" he asks, "and longs to see good days" (Ps 33:13; RB Prol.15). He quickly follows with a second question. "Who shall dwell in Your tent, or who shall rest on Your holy

8. Marie-Bernard de Soos, "What Is Benedictine Spirituality?" in *Saint Benedict of Nursia*, 29.

mountain?" (Ps 14.1; RB Prol.23). The answer to both questions? Keep your tongue from evil, do good, seek after peace (Ps 13:14-15). Do justice, speak truth, praise God (Ps 14:2-4). Psalm 113 provides the key to life shaped by and lived in the gospel: "Not to us, O God, not to us; but to Your name give glory" (Ps 113:9; RB Prol.30). Benedict demonstrates how the fundamental questions of life are answered by the single gospel-word: humility. In his chapter on humility (RB 7), it should be no surprise that Benedict illustrates the twelve steps to perfect love with no less than sixteen quotations from the Psalms.

Let's not forget that the Psalms have served as the primary song-book for the Jewish and Christian communities for nearly three thousand years. I think that defines the test of time. Esther de Waal explains why they have been so central:

> The psalms are the songs of a journeying people, and I can identify in them many of my feelings on my own journey to God. They express hope, fear, anger, delight. They are wonderfully honest. Sometimes they seem like incantations lulling me into the certainty of the goodness of God. Sometimes they are battle hymns that will not let me forget the tremendous battle against the forces of evil that surround me. Sometimes God is close, sometimes God is distant. Sometimes they speak of fullness and riches, at other times they come out of poverty and emptiness. . . . Saying the psalms day in and day out, for year after year after year, no matter how I feel, unites me with thousands of men and women across all divides of time and place who have shared them with me.[9]

Given the profound and formative nature of these prayers, Benedict's expectation was that his monastics would pray the entirety of the Psalter every week.[10] In order to give the Psalms an honored place in monastic life, he developed a meticulous way of reciting the Psalms together in the Daily Office (RB 8-19). I can only imagine that

---

9. de Waal, *A Life-giving Way*, 60.

10. With the reforms of Vatican II, many monastic communities engage the Psalms in a variety of modified schedules. For a helpful exploration of various practices, see Eric Dean, "Singing the Psalms," in *Saint Benedict for the Laity* (Collegeville, MN: Liturgical Press, 1989), 41–47.

many monastics have sung the entire Psalter by heart. It has become their heart language.

In my journey as an oblate, the Psalms that have always interested me the most are those that Benedict established as a foundation for the *horarium*, as it is called. Those Psalms that I have recited daily continue to shape me definitively. I think, for instance, of Psalm 95 (the Venite), which opens Vigils or Morning Prayer. The simple acclamation, "O come, let us sing to the Lord," reminds me daily that life is a song to be sung. Thanksgiving and joy are the keynotes of this song because "we are God's people." Psalm 63—included in Morning Prayer on special days—inspires me to long for God when my spirit is like a "dry, warm, waterless land." It reminds me that nothing is more important than God's gracious, sustaining presence. Psalm 51 is also a staple of Morning Prayer. "Have mercy on me, O God," I plead, "according to your steadfast love. Create in me a clean heart, O God, and put a new and right spirit within me." This Psalm reminds me that God envelopes my brokenness and failure in forgiving and transforming love. Psalm 134 at Compline or Evening Prayer reminds me that I bless things by declaring God blessed: "Come, bless the Lord, all you servants of the Lord. . . . The Lord who made heaven and earth give you blessing out of Zion." I have used the phrase "remind me" here repeatedly, intentionally. The Psalms help me to remember and therefore to praise God. Singing the Psalms ultimately fills my heart with praise.

"[Benedict] wanted the 'music' of the psalms to enter the minds and hearts of all," proclaims Demetrius Dumm, "so that their cadences would become like a familiar tune that one cannot stop humming."[11] This brings me back to David Steindl-Rast's *The Music of Silence*. Remember, I am talking here about sacred song, so I want to draw on a number of insights from this book that have meant so much to me over the years. First, in chanting the Psalms, nothing stands between you and God. A part of the beauty of chant is the fact that it is free. It simply follows the natural cadence of the words. It opens a space in which you can abide with Christ.

Second, this engagement with the Psalms helps us find the elusive

---

11. Dumm, *Cherish Christ Above All*, 124.

now dimension of our lives. It calls us out of the normal ordering of time (*chronos*) in which "now" is seldom located and leads us into the "eternal now" (*chairos*). It enables us to taste and celebrate the joy and beauty of life and the glory of God right now. I can remember "times" when "time stood still" as I was singing.

Third, chanting is not a solo performance; it is a community action. Even the antiphonal nature of chanting (which gave shape to the "choir" in church architecture) accentuates its communal dimension. Psalm-chanting is "an expression of spiritual life as a whole, which is, in its essence, a life of love, of listening and responding to God and to one another. Love is not a solo act."[12]

John and Charles Wesley prayed the Psalms regularly in Morning and Evening Prayer. A musical setting of Psalm 130 at a service of Evensong at St. Paul's Cathedral even figured prominently in John Wesley's conversion. Charles Wesley prepared lyrical paraphrases of nearly all the Psalms.[13] His practice of the Psalms reflects many of Benedict's values. He saw the gospel in the Psalms. He appreciated the heartfelt nature of these prayers—their honesty and humanity. He found ways to help the Psalms speak to his own world. He used these prayers to introduce seekers to God and to offer guidance to Christ's disciples.[14] The Psalms shaped the Wesleys, but Charles Wesley's production of English hymns changed his world and ours.

Hymns and Spiritual Songs

"Before we reached the place," Grace Murray recalls, "we heard the people singing hymns. The very sound set all my passions afloat, though I did not know one word they uttered, which plainly shows how the affections may be greatly moved while the understanding is quite dark."[15]

---

12. David Steindl-Rast, *The Music of Silence: Entering the Sacred Space of Monastic Experience* (San Francisco: HarperSanFrancisco, 1995), 9.

13. See Paul W. Chilcote, *Sheltering with the Psalms: 30 Days of Prayer with Charles Wesley* (Cleveland, TN: Aldersgate Press, 2021).

14. See S T Kimbrough Jr., "Directions of Interpretation in Charles Wesley's Psalm Poetry," *Proceedings of The Charles Wesley Society* 16 (2012): 29–59.

15. William Bennet, ed., *Memoirs of Grace Bennet* (Macclesfield: E. Bayley, 1803), 213.

This reference to the important role that hymns played in the Wesleyan movement is typical. Methodists sang the keynotes of their heritage in a unique and winsome lyrical spirituality. The Wesleys revolutionized Anglican worship with the rediscovery of congregational singing. "The eighteenth-century revival," Richard Heitzenrater observes, "was to a great extent borne on the wings of Charles' poetry. Charles' hymns not only helped form the texture of the Methodist mind but also, perhaps more importantly, set the temper of the Methodist spirit."[16]

The hymns themselves were a powerful tool in the Spirit's work of revival and shaped the spirituality of the Methodist people perhaps more than any other single source besides the Bible. The singing of hymns and spiritual songs, in other words, played a critical role in the development of Wesleyan spirituality. In this regard, the hymns formed the singers in three particular ways that align closely with the purposes of chanting the Psalms in the Benedictine tradition. The hymn functions as promise, as catalyst, and as the language of the heart.[17]

Promise. In the Wesleyan way, hymns reinforce the fundamental idea of promise, both God's to us and ours to God. Charles Wesley's hymns frequently remind the singer of God's faithfulness—a sign or seal of God's promise. In her journal, Hester Ann Rogers reveled in God's promises revealed in a favorite hymn sung in community worship:

> Reading the word of God in private this day was an unspeakable blessing. O! how precious are the promises. What a depth in these words: "For all the promises of God in him are yea, and in him, amen, unto the glory of God." Yes, my soul, they are so to thee! The Father delights to fulfil, and the Spirit to seal them on my heart. O that dear invaluable truth!
>
> > Ready art thou to receive;
> > Readier is thy God to give.

---

16. Quoted in S T Kimbrough Jr., *Lost in Wonder* (Nashville: The Upper Room, 1987), 11–12.

17. The following paragraphs draw heavily from my essay "Songs of the Heart: Hymn Allusions in the Writings of Early Methodist Women," *Proceedings of the Charles Wesley Society* 5 (1998): 99–114.

The Lord poured his love abundantly into my soul while worshiping before him. And I was enabled to renew my covenant, to be wholly and for ever his!"[18]

The stanza that follows Hester's allusion celebrates the peace and joy promised to the faithful disciple and forms these qualities in the spirit of the singer united to God through Christ:

> Abba, Father! Hear Thy child,
> Late in Jesus reconciled!
> Hear, and all the graces shower,
> All the joy, and peace, and power,
> All my Savior asks above,
> All the life and heaven of love.[19]

Catalyst. The singing of hymns also functions as a catalyst for transformation, conversion, and spiritual renewal. One Methodist woman encountered Christ anew at a celebration of Holy Communion on Easter Eve. A hymn consummated the promise from Jesus that she sought:

Just as I came to the rails, the family sang and God spoke the words to my soul,

> Lift your eyes of faith, and look
>   To the signs he did ordain!
> Thus the bread of Life was broke!
>   Thus the Lamb of God was slain!
> Thus was shed on Calvary,
>   His last drop of blood for *thee*![20]

---

18. Hester Ann Rogers, *An Account of the Experience of Hester Ann Rogers* (New York: Hunt & Eaton, 1893), 132.

19. Wesley, *Hymns and Sacred Poems* (1739), 219–20.

20. "An Account of Mrs. Sarah Ryan," *Arminian Magazine* 2 (1779): 304; Wesley, *Hymns on the Lord's Supper* (1745), 89.

J. Ernest Rattenbury describes the following stanza of a Charles Wesley hymn as the "Protestant Crucifix."[21] Singing this hymn changed lives and opened the hearts of many to Christ:

> Never love nor sorrow was
> Like that my Jesus showed;
> See Him stretched on yonder cross,
>   And crushed beneath our load!
> Now discern the Deity,
>   Now His heavenly birth declare;
> Faith cries out, 'Tis He, 'tis He,
>   My God, that suffers there![22]

Heart-language. Hymn singing shaped a Wesleyan language of the heart. In my own experience, singing about the mystery of God often supersedes the inadequacy of my words. When I am overwhelmed by a sense of God's presence or rejoice over the gift of overflowing love, I turn to song. In either case, it is the language of the heart filled with love—filled with God. Singing hymns and sacred texts continues to give Methodist people a lyrical vocabulary to express their experience of God's love, and the experience of this love is often mediated in the singing in which they share together. Praise and prayer, grace and promise all combine in Isabella Wilson's bursting heart of faith:

> Oh! the unbounded love of Jesus to my soul. His promises are all precious. My peace flows as a river while he teaches me the lessons of his grace, of faith and holiness. My soul is athirst for all the mind that was in him.

> Lord, take my heart and let it be
>   For ever closed to all but thee:
>   Seal thou my breast, and let me wear
>   That pledge of love for ever there.[23]

---

21. J. Ernest Rattenbury, *The Eucharistic Hymns of John and Charles Wesley* (London: Epworth Press, 1948), 153.

22. Wesley, *Hymns on the Lord's Supper*, 16.

23. John Pipe, "Memoir of Miss Isabella Wilson," *Methodist Magazine* (31): 564; Wesley, *Hymns and Sacred Poems* (1740), 75.

The weekend I was completing my work on this chapter I also participated in the closing events of our Bach Festival season. Our final concert was an amazing collection of compositions built around the theme "The Pursuit of Peace." We opened with a Ukrainian prayer. Its magnificent harmonies and modulations explored the depth and range of the human voice at a hum. Almost all the songs we sang were sacred texts, including the magnificent prayer of St. Francis of Assisi. Karl Jenkins's stunningly powerful "The Armed Man: A Mass for Peace" filled the second half of the concert, carrying us musically through the tragedy and horror of war into a hope-filled space in which our voices rang with the joy of peace. Several words linger in my heart and mind to this day: humanity, empathy, peace. Singing these sacred songs reminded me in deeply moving ways that we are called to be people of peace. In a world torn apart by anger, violence, and war, God calls us to sow seeds of reconciliation, peace, and love. The music and the words—even the sounds we created—spoke peace into the hearts of everyone involved.

The three statements at the head of this chapter invite us to sing with gratitude in our hearts, to sing with our minds in harmony with our voices, and to open our hearts to learn the new, the gospel song of love. Nothing is more central to the Benedictine Wesleyan way than singing the faith.

* * *

A Biblical Treasure

In Paul's portrait of the ideal family of God, note his allusions to harmony, psalms, hymns, and spiritual songs, all bound together by love and gratitude.

> Above all, clothe yourselves with love, which binds everything together in perfect harmony. And let the peace of Christ rule in your hearts, to which indeed you were called in one body. And be thankful. Let the word of Christ dwell in you richly; teach and admonish one another in all wisdom; and with gratitude in your hearts sing psalms, hymns, and spiritual songs to God. (Colossians 3:14-16)

A Benedictine Treasure

God blessed Hildegard of Bingen with many gifts, but none has captured the imagination of so many as her music. She expressed the inexpressible sweetness of love primarily through her song. In this brief prayer, she celebrates what could be called the music of the spheres.

> To the Trinity be praise!
> God is music, God is life
> that nurtures every creature in its kind.
> Our God is the song of the angel throng
> and the splendor of secret ways
> hid from all humankind.
> But God our life is the life of all.
> To the Trinity be praise!
> It is sound and life and creator
> of all beings in their life.
> It is the praise of the angelic host
> and the wondrous splendor of mysteries
> unknown to humankind.
> It is the life in all. Amen.[24]

A Wesleyan Treasure

Nothing inspired Charles Wesley more than a community of God's people singing together. In this hymn he conceives the community of God's people as a choir engaged in perpetual praise of God.

> Thou God of harmony and love,
> Whose name transports the saints above,
>   And lulls the ravished spheres,
> Teach me the new, the gospel song,
> And let my hand, my heart, my tongue
>   Move only to thy praise.

---

24. Hildegard of Bingen, *Symphonia: A Critical Edition of the "Symphonia Armonie Celestium Revelationum" (Symphony of the Harmony of Celestial Revelations)*, ed. Barbara Newman (Ithaca, NY: Cornell University Press, 1998), 142–43.

Jesus! The heaven of heavens he is,
The soul of harmony and bliss!
>> And while on him we gaze,
And while his glorious voice we hear,
Our spirits are all eye, all ear,
>> And silence speaks his praise.

O might I die that awe to prove,
That prostrate awe which dares not move
>> Before the great Three-One,
To shout by turns the bursting joy,
And all eternity employ
>> In songs around the throne.[25]

---

25. Wesley, *Redemption Hymns*, 34–36.

PART 3

COMMON GOALS OF LIFE TOGETHER

Chapter 7

Humility

He humbled himself and became obedient to the point of death.
—Philippians 2:8
The first step of humility is obedience without delay. —Benedict
Now, one of the chief properties of love is humility. —John Wesley

I have told the following story many times because it has been so formative in my life. I was taking a class on Howard Thurman as a student at Duke Divinity School. Thurman had exerted a major influence on the life of Dr. Martin Luther King Jr., so he was of great interest to me. About halfway through the semester, my classmates and I were sitting in our small seminar room waiting for class to begin. The door opened and in walked Howard Thurman. It was as though someone turned on the lights as he came into the room. Thurman radiated God's love. I will never forget that moment.

In addition to his radiant countenance, I remember his deep humility. He communicated that humility by the way he related to each of us. It was as though he was visiting our class because he felt privileged to share his time with us. Our professor invited him to say a few words about himself. "Oh no," he retorted. "I'd much rather learn something about each of these fine students. I'm more interested in knowing about them than in talking about me." It was clear that he meant what he said. The topic of discussion for the class was "truth," and he revealed something to me quite profound that day. He demonstrated how relationships—and particularly the posture we assume in our relationships in life—shape our world. I still remember him saying something to the effect that the ultimate test of your truth is the humility it inspires.

When class was over, Thurman said goodbye to each of us by name. We all felt, I am sure, that he really knew us and that we had a new friend. He is one of the most humble persons I have ever met.

A Benedictine Wesleyan way seeks to cultivate a spirit and posture of humility—the first of three goals held in common by both traditions. One of the invaluable lessons I have learned in my journey with Benedict and the Wesleys is the foundational role of this virtue in life. Indeed, as all the great saints of the church have demonstrated, only humility provides an effective antidote to the debilitating disease of human pride: hubris. Humility is the key to the Christian life. This chapter revolves around three important facets of the practice of humility. The Wesleys and Benedict take their ultimate clues from the life of Christ, the self-emptying servant. First and foremost, we have a model of humility in Christ and his teachings. Benedict developed a twelve-rung ladder of humility that leads, he believed, to perfect love. As a central part of Benedictine spirituality, these twelve steps merit our scrutiny. In order to cultivate this virtue in our lives we must assume the posture of humility. This orientation to God and others enables us to experience the inexpressible sweetness of love.

Banquets and the Model of Christ

Jesus's parable of the wedding banquet (Luke 14:7-14) provides a potent narrative illustration of the interconnected nature of humility and gratitude as well as humility and hospitality.[1] Jesus tells this story when he notices guests beginning to jockey their way into positions of honor in the hall.

> "Go and sit down at the lowest place, so that when your host comes, he may say to you, 'Friend, move up higher'; then you will be honored in the presence of all who sit at the table with you. For all who exalt themselves will be humbled, and those who humble themselves will be exalted." (10–11)

---

1. We will explore the second common goal of the Benedictine Wesleyan way, hospitality, in the next chapter.

Note the intimate connections among grace, gratitude, thanksgiving, and humility. The dispositions of gratitude and humility go hand in hand. You cannot express gratitude to yourself! Your gratitude reflects your understanding that relationships define who you are. Gratitude only happens in relation to others. Your expressions of appreciation for others sow the seed of humility in your life.

Luke places another parable immediately after this meal story in the narrative flow of his Gospel—the parable of the great dinner (Luke 14:15-24). The main theme of this story is joy, the sheer joy of receiving an invitation. God reaches out to us in our need. We come to the table because we are hungry. All people hunger—all of us some of the time, and some of us all the time. Those who have little testify to the indignity and pervasiveness of hunger. The rich starve inwardly, while appearing fat and satisfied on the outside. We hear echoes here of Mary's Song from the opening chapter of Luke's Gospel: "He has brought down the powerful from their thrones and lifted up the lowly; he has filled the hungry with good things and sent the rich away empty" (Luke 1:52-53). Acknowledgment of your own need also sows the seed of humility in your life.

The lesson of these meal stories is clear. The greatest in God's eyes are those who consider themselves to be the least—those who live in genuine mutuality with others as beloved siblings.

Christ models this kind of humility. He demonstrates the profoundly relational nature of humility through his actions. In his letter to the Philippians, Paul reminds the community to imitate the Christ of whom they sang in one of the earliest hymns of the church:

> Let the same mind be in you that was in Christ Jesus,
> who, though he existed in the form of God,
> did not regard equality with God as something to be grasped,
> but emptied himself,
> taking the form of a slave, assuming human likeness.
> And being found in appearance as a human.
> he humbled himself
> and became obedient to the point of death—
> even death on a cross.

Therefore God exalted him even more highly
    and gave him the name,
      that is above every other name,
so that at the name given to Jesus
    every knee should bend,
      in heaven and on earth and under the earth,
and every tongue should confess
    that Jesus Christ is Lord,
      to the glory of God the Father. (Phil 2:5-11)

This hymn combines the theme of humility with the act of self-emptying (*kenosis*). Jesus "emptied himself, taking the form of a slave"; he "humbled himself."

Charles Wesley's most profound exposition of this kenotic theme comes in a hymn exploring the titles of Christ. It is essentially a lyrical paraphrase of the hymn cited by Paul:

Arise, my soul, arise,
    Thy Savior's sacrifice!
All the names that love could find,
    All the forms that love could take,
Jesus in himself has joined,
    Thee, my soul, his own to make.

Equal with God, most high,
    He laid his glory by:
He, the eternal God was born,
    Man with men he deigned to appear,
Object of his creature's scorn,
    Pleased a servant's form to wear.

He left his throne above
    Emptied of all, but love:
Whom the heavens cannot contain
    God vouchsafed a worm to appear,

Lord of glory, *Son of man,*
> Poor, and vile, and abject here.[2]

Humility and self-emptying are distinct, but inseparable in the example of Christ. The root from which the word *humility* comes literally means "dirt" (*humus*).[3] In the Incarnation God literally humbles God's self to the dust. Wesley provides here a portrait of a God who "laid his glory by." This God is the Eternal "contracted to a span." God stoops down and condescends. God, in other words, comes down to the human level, enters into this world, and demonstrates the lengths to which love will go to establish and nurture relationships of love. In many of his hymns, Charles condenses the whole wonder of Christ's humility into a single line: "He emptied himself of all but love."[4]

Toward the end of the Rule, Benedict returns to the theme of humility. Quoting Romans 12:10 he says, "Each should try to be the first to honor the other" (RB 72:4). "No one," he continues, "is to pursue what is judged better for one's self, but rather what is better for others. They are to show to one another the purest love" (RB 72:7-8). Humility has to do with lifting other people up. Humble people relinquish the need to dominate others or to win. They don't wield their power against others. They don't weaponize their faith or fixate on their need to be right. Jesus promoted a vision of life in which we find inner peace and outflowing love by elevating others.

Benedict's Ladder of Humility

The monastic heritage elevates a lofty vision with regards to life in Christ—the life of a child of God in community. Benedict's vision

---

2. Wesley, *Hymns and Sacred Poems* (1739), 165–67. Just to give you a sense of Wesley's pervasive use of Phil 2:5-11, and therefore its centrality, see the allusions to this text in John Wesley, *The Works of John Wesley*, vol. 7, *A Collection of Hymns for the Use of the People Called Methodists*, ed. Franz Hildebrandt and Oliver A. Beckerlegge (Nashville: Abingdon Press, 1989), 101, 108, 118, 193, 197, 246, 265, 315–16, 421, 476, 507, 508, 520, 522, 524, 527, 531, 534, 577, 626, 644, 678, 697, 710.
3. See de Waal, *Living with Contradiction*, 97–98.
4. Wesley, *Hymns and Sacred Poems* (1739), 118.

of harmony, wholeness, and balance culminates in humility—a value or virtue that liberates the self to love as Christ has loved. He established his monastic communities to help men and women grow more fully into the image of Christ—to love as he loves, in humility with peace of heart. It is not surprising, therefore, that Benedict devotes the entirety of a chapter to humility, the longest chapter of his Rule (RB 7). Whereas he commits five paragraphs to the matter of obedience (RB 5, 71), he deliberates over the practice of humility in no less that twenty (RB 7). The life of humility to which he aspired himself continues to be one of the most important goals of all Benedictine monastics.

In my discussion of harmony in chapter 3, I used one of Benedict's primary images related to humility—sometimes called the ladder of humility—to illustrate balance in his spirituality. I want to spend more time here reflecting on his words about humility and his "twelve steps of humility" in particular. This is of special importance to me because this path of humility has helped me accept my gifts and talents joyfully while letting go of my false self that often seeks to be in competition with others. Comparison is the downfall of us all. At a conference related to monasticism years ago I remember someone saying that humility helps us become more authentically, beautifully, and lovingly human. This expresses the Benedictine legacy well. Benedict does not view humility as an abstract idea; rather, humility is an enacted and habituated posture that enables us to love God, others, and ourselves more fully.

As you can well imagine, much ink has been spilled over the years with regards to Benedict's words and images associated with humility and his twelve steps.[5] In one of her many discussions of humility, Sister Joan distills Benedict's twelve degrees of humility into six basic propositions:

---

5. Of the many books that reflect on Benedict's ladder of humility and its twelve steps, I recommend Michael Casey, *Truthful Living: Saint Benedict's Teaching on Humility* (Leominster: Gracewing, 2001); Aquinata Börkmann, *From the Tools of Good Works to the Heart of Humility* (Collegeville, MN: Liturgical Press, 2017); and J. Augustine Wetta, *Saint Benedict's Twelve-Step Guide to Genuine Self-Esteem* (San Francisco: Ignatian Press, 2017). Of special interest is the audio recording of Thomas Merton, *12 Degrees of Humility* (Chevy Chase, MD: Now You Know Media, 2012).

1. The presence of God demands total response.
2. Not pride, but the desire to be God, is the opposite of humility.
3. Spiritual development is not an event, it is a process.
4. Humility frees the spirit; it does not batter it.
5. Humility is the glue of our relationships.
6. Self-love can destroy the self. [6]

I summarize the twelve steps myself with the following admonitions: If you aspire to humility, practice acknowledging God's majesty, accepting God's will, receiving others' direction, countenancing others' ideas, confessing your sin, embracing menial tasks, receiving others' criticism, learning from others, bridling your tongue, curbing your frivolity, minimizing your words, and embodying your humility.[7] At the conclusion of Benedict's exposition of humility, he offers the only promise in his Rule: "Having, therefore, ascended all these steps of humility; they will presently arrive at the perfect love of God which casts out fear" (RB 7:67).

Having spent a good amount of time studying and attempting to live into Benedict's twelve steps of humility as best I can, I believe he viewed them primarily in relational categories. The first two steps describe the practice of humility in relation to God. The remaining steps deal with humility in two other relational senses—in terms of our relationships with others and in terms of our relationship with our inner self. While there is no clear hierarchical model at play in Benedict's ordering of these steps, there is a sense that the first two steps provide the essential foundation. If we begin this journey alienated from God, then we will never progress further. In this fundamental relationship of our lives, we must acknowledge God's majesty (1) and accept God's will (2). Everything depends on our ability to let God be

---

6. Chittister, *Wisdom Distilled*, 53–56.

7. Esther de Waal has her own interpretive framework: "The first seven steps look at the growth of the interior dispositions, the next five at the exterior conduct" (*Seeking God*, 46). Augustine Wetta attempts to reduce each step to one term: fear of God, self-denial, obedience, perseverance, repentance, serenity, self-abasement, prudence, silence, dignity, discretion, and reverence (*Humility Rules*). Cf. Tomaine, *The Rule of Benedict*, 153–71.

God; that ability is, in itself, God's gracious gift. Awareness of God—in other words, God's loving presence, power, and purpose—facilitates our ascent.

With regards to our relationships with others, I believe all four steps in this sphere fall under the umbrella of one word: *teachability*. To be humble means to be teachable. We must be willing to receive guidance (3), ideas (4), criticism (7), and instruction (8) from others. The word *disciple* means "learner." We sit at Jesus's feet. "If you, even you," he sighs, "had only recognized on this day the things that make for peace!" (Luke 19:42). God longs to teach us the way of righteousness, peace, and joy (Rom 14:17). We simply need ears that can hear and hearts ready to respond. With regards to our inner selves, we must learn to confess (5), to work (6), and to demonstrate self-control (9, 10, 11). The fullest possible transparency characterizes the life of the truly humble person. Living in such a way that our outer self and our inner self are completely in sync is the greatest challenge of life. True humility can be seen by others through our words, actions, and particularly by the way we relate to others (12). All Benedict's steps of humility, essentially, boil down to three critical words: awareness, teachability, and self-knowledge.

The Posture of Humility

What is a posture of humility? How do you assume it? First and foremost, I am using the term here in an active and relational way. Posture is not something passive or theoretical. It has to do with your primary orientation to God and others and how this makes you behave. While carrying with it the connotation of a physical position—like Mary sitting at Jesus's feet or Jesus kneeling at the feet of his disciples—it also implies an attitude or disposition. In this sense, you position yourself in a particular way relationally. You can then either maintain the posture (something I find quite difficult to do) or fall out of it (something much easier). To sustain the posture of humility requires practice and discipline. The Wesleys and Benedict have taught me three important lessons about the practice and posture of humility. First, you have to cultivate humility. Second, humility is best nurtured through the imitation of Christ. Third, you practice humility through your actions.

Cultivation. A Benedictine Wesleyan way teaches that you must cultivate the virtue of humility—the anchor of your soul. No one is born humble; humility does not simply arise or emerge in your life without intention. Benedict instructed his monks to practice the twelve steps for the purpose of cultivating humility in their lives. The daily commitment to live humbly is critical. Samuel and Susanna Wesley sought to cultivate humility among their children. The writings of John Worthington, one example among many, were favorites in this regard. In one of his most famous books, *The Great Duty of Self-Resignation to the Divine Will*, he discusses how humility predisposes our hearts to repentance, patience, gratitude, faith, and love.[8] Humility is the virtue upon which all other virtues are built. The Wesley parents reminded their children about the dangers of pride and encouraged them to nurture humility in their hearts.

Benedict's twelve steps and his statements about humility in general point to the importance of this kind of intentional discipleship. In the chapter on community above I shared some thoughts with you about "mutual accountability." Neither Benedict nor the Wesleys would ever have conceived humility possible apart from this gift we offer to one another. In this regard, the practice of obedience plays a major role in both traditions.[9] Indeed, all forms of accountability entail obedience. Benedict claims that "the first step of humility is obedience without delay, which is characteristic of those who cherish Christ above all else" (RB 5:1). John Wesley reflects on humility in a sermon on Jesus's promise, "blessed are the poor in spirit" (Matt 5:3). Those who are humble—that is, who are obedient to the will of God and the law of love—"have that disposition of heart which is the first step to all real,

---

8. This classic text is still available today: John Worthington, *The Great Duty of Self-Resignation to the Divine Will* (Farmington Hills, MI: Gale ECCO Print Editions, 2010). An Anglican academic of the seventeenth century, he served as master of Jesus College, Cambridge.

9. See the interesting discussions of the relation between obedience and humility in Chittister, *Wisdom Distilled*, 133–46; Stewart, *Prayer and Community*, 53–70; and Dean, *Saint Benedict for the Laity*, 33–40.

substantial happiness, either in this world or that which is to come."[10] Obedience and accountability nurture poverty of spirit.

Imitation. A Benedictine Wesleyan way teaches that the best way to cultivate humility is to imitate Christ. The devotional classic of Thomas à Kempis, *The Imitation of Christ*, shaped John and Charles Wesley's view of the Christian life profoundly.[11] The theme of humility pervades this spiritual manual for the Christian pilgrimage. At the very outset Thomas links a biblical admonition to this central quality of authentic Christian discipleship: "True self-knowledge is the highest and most profitable discovery in life. Do not think of yourself, therefore, more highly than you ought and always think well and highly of others" (I.2).[12]

> If you think you know a lot, acknowledge that there are many more things about which you know nothing. Do not let your knowledge turn you into an arrogant person; rather, admit your own ignorance. Those who aspire to be wise seek to nurture a spirit of humility in their lives. (I.2)

We usually think of imitation in the sense of observing and replicating the behavior of some other person. While Benedict makes no explicit reference to the imitation of Christ in the Rule, he and the Wesleys most certainly have this in mind. On its most basic level, imitation of Christ means to live a Christlike life. But this means much more than simply mimicking Jesus; it means having his mind and spirit. To return to the kenotic hymn of Paul, it means "having the mind of Christ" (see Phil 2:5)—cultivating a spirit like that of Jesus. Clearly, humility is an attitude or an attribute, but the Benedictine Wesleyan way has also taught me that it is an action. Humble actions

---

10. Wesley, *Works*, 1:476.

11. John Wesley considered *The Imitation of Christ* to be of such great importance that he produced some 120 editions in four different forms during his lifetime. He carried a copy of his own 1741 pocket edition in his saddlebag for half a century, until his death. See Paul W. Chilcote, *The Imitation of Christ: Selections Annotated & Explained* (Woodstock, VT: SkyLight Paths, 2012), xi.

12. Quoted in Chilcote, *Imitation of Christ*, 5. All quotations from the *Imitation* are cited from this edition.

that are Christlike flow out of a posture of humility. In a lyrical para-phrase of James 1:27, Charles Wesley binds the "mind" of Philippians 2 to the faith-filled "action" of James:

> To me, for Jesu's sake, impart,
>> And plant thy nature in my heart.
>
> Thy mind throughout my life be shown,
>> While listening to the wretch's cry,
> The widow's and the orphan's groan,
>> On mercy's wings I swiftly fly
> The poor and helpless to relieve,
>> My life, my all for them to give.[13]

Action. The Benedictine Wesleyan way teaches that we are called to practice humility through concrete actions. In the life of Christ, nowhere was his humble love manifest more poignantly than in the Upper Room. Here, among his closest friends, Jesus translates humility into a profound sign-act of servant ministry. He washes the disciples' feet (John 13:1-20). He demonstrates the paradoxical lesson that great-ness in the community of his disciples is measured by one's willingness to serve.[14] Jesus left no doubt that he—the chief of all servants—invites all into the ministry of humble, self-emptying love. In one of Charles Wesley's hymns based on the foot-washing episode in John 13, all these themes converge into a compelling portrait of humility:

> Jesu, by highest heavens adored,
>> The church's glorious Head;
> With humble joy I call Thee, Lord,
>> And in Thy footsteps tread.
>
> At charity's almighty call
>> I lay my greatness by,

---

13. Wesley, *Scripture Hymns*, 2:380.

14. See my treatment of this *diakonia* theme in Wesleyan theology in Paul W. Chilcote, *Recapturing the Wesleys' Vision: An Introduction to the Faith of John and Charles Wesley* (Downers Grove, IL: IVP Academic, 2004), 91–118.

The least of saints, I wait on all,
    Through humble actions fly.

Happy, if I their grief may cheer,
    And mitigate their pain,
And wait upon the servants here,
    To extend my Master's reign.[15]

To translate humility into action—to have the same mind that was in Christ (Phil 2:5), to grow into "the measure of the full stature of Jesus" (Eph 4:13), to become a letter of Jesus written on the tablet of the human heart (2 Cor 3:3)—means to become like Christ in his obedience, humility, and loving action. Humility equates, in the end, to actions rooted in love. Mary Hanson, an early Methodist woman, turned all these profound insights into a prayer.

O, blessed fountain of love! Fill my heart more with your divine principle. Sink me lower in the depths of humility, and let me sit at the feet of Jesus, and learn of him. Enlarge my soul, that I may better contemplate your glory. And may I prove myself your child, by bearing a resemblance to you, my heavenly Father, through the disposition of my heart and the action of my hands![16]

The Benedictine Wesleyan way invites us to embrace the posture of humility expressed through the human kindness of hospitality.

* * *

A Biblical Treasure

In Philippians 2 Paul is quoting one of the earliest hymns of the Christian community. This sacred song celebrates the humility of Christ and his model of self-sacrificial love.

---

15. Wesley, *Hymns and Sacred Poems* (1749), 1:213–14, adapted.

16. Quoted in Adam Clarke, *Memoirs of the Late Eminent Mrs. Mary Cooper, of London* (Halifax: William Nicholson and Sons, c. 1822), 170–71. Cf. Manuela Scheiba, "Learning to Pray: A Journey Through Benedict's Chapter on Humility," *The American Benedictine Review* 64, no. 2 (June 2013): 118–37.

Let the same mind be in you that was in Christ Jesus, who, though he existed in the form of God, did not regard equality with God as something to be grasped, but emptied himself, taking the form of a slave, assuming human likeness. And being found in appearance as a human, he humbled himself and became obedient to the point of death—even death on a cross. Therefore God exalted him even more highly and gave him the name, that is above every other name, so that at the name given to Jesus every knee should bend, in heaven and on earth and under the earth, and every tongue should confess that Jesus Christ is Lord, to the glory of God the Father. (Phil 2:5-11)

A Benedictine Treasure

Thomas Merton, one of the most noteworthy spiritual guides of our time and a Trappist monk, disarms us with his honesty. His life and this prayer demonstrate the intimate connection between humility and trust in God.

My Lord God, I have no idea where I am going. I do not see the road ahead of me. I cannot know for certain where it will end. Nor do I really know myself, and the fact that I think I am following Your will does not mean that I am actually doing so. But I believe that the desire to please You does in fact please You. And I hope I have that desire in all that I am doing. I hope that I will never do anything apart from that desire. And I know that, if I do this, You will lead me by the right road, though I may know nothing about it. Therefore I will trust You always though I may seem to be lost and in the shadow of death. I will not fear, for You are ever with me, and You will never leave me to face my perils alone. Amen.

A Wesleyan Treasure

In this hymn, Charles Wesley reflects on the mystery of the Incarnation and the lengths to which the God of love will go to reach out to us. Our imitation of Christ's humility reaches out as well so that all may know of God's goodness and love.

Arise, my soul, arise,
    Thy Saviour's sacrifice!
All the names that love could find,
    All the forms that love could take,
Jesus in himself has joined,
    Thee, my soul, his own to make.

Equal with God most high,
    He laid his glory by:
He the eternal God was born,
    Man with men he deigned to appear,
Object of his creature's scorn,
    Pleased a servant's form to wear.

He left his throne above,
    Emptied of all but love:
Whom the heavens cannot contain,
    God vouchsafed a worm to appear,
Lord of glory, Son of man,
    Poor, and vile, and abject here.[17]

Chapter 8

Hospitality

Do not neglect to show hospitality to strangers. —*Hebrews 13:2*
All guests who present themselves are to be welcomed as Christ. —*Benedict*
Come, sinners, to the gospel feast, / Let every soul be Jesus' guest.
—*Charles Wesley*

We never really know who we are entertaining. "I was a stranger," Christ declares, "and you welcomed me" (Matt 25:35). One of my favorite stories illustrates how a couple took hospitality to strangers with utmost seriousness. You may recognize the name Jürgen Moltmann, a name synonymous with the "theology of hope."[1] I first met Professor Moltmann when I was a graduate student at Duke University. During one of his visits to campus, I invited him to lunch and we enjoyed a wonderful meal together. While introducing myself more fully, I explained that I was working in my doctoral studies with Frank Baker. "Oh," he interrupted, "would you like to hear a story about Frank and Nellie Baker?"

He said that during the Second World War there was a German prisoner of war camp on the northeast coast of England. A young pastor and his wife served a small Methodist circuit close by. Out of a deep sense of compassion they felt compelled to do something to reach out to the German soldiers who were so despised throughout the region. They mustered up their courage and made an appointment to meet

---

1. See Jürgen Moltmann, *Theology of Hope*, trans. James W. Leitch (London: SCM Press, 1967); and *Ethics of Hope*, trans. Margaret Kohl (Minneapolis: Fortress Press, 2012).

with the commander of the facility. They shared their plan with him and requested permission to take a prisoner with them to church each Sunday and then to their home where they would eat their Sunday dinner together. To their utter astonishment, he agreed. So Sunday by Sunday, a steady flow of German prisoners worshiped and ate with the Bakers in their home throughout the course of the war. This world-famous theologian paused, looked at me intently, and said, "One of those soldiers was a young man by the name of Jürgen Moltmann, and it was at Frank and Nellie Baker's Sunday dinner table that the seed of hope was planted in my soul."[2]

My abbey includes hospitality among its seven rich ways: "St. Benedict tells his monks that 'all guests who arrive shall be received as Christ' (RB 53). This spiritual intuition, that Christ himself is present in the person of the guest, undergirds the monastery's unconditional welcome of all guests and its reverse for them."[3] Henri Nouwen, in his devotional classic titled *Reaching Out*, describes three important movements in the spiritual life. One of these movements involves a transformational journey from hostility to hospitality. I am still drawn to one of his particularly poignant statements:

> Our society seems to be increasingly full of fearful, defensive, ag-gressive people anxiously clinging to their property and inclined to look at their surrounding world with suspicion, always expecting an enemy to suddenly appear, intrude and do harm. But still—that is our vocation: to convert the *hostis* into a *hospes*, the enemy into a guest and to create the free and fearless space where brotherhood and sisterhood can be formed and fully experienced.[4]

---

2. See Paul W. Chilcote, *Active Faith: Resisting 4 Dangerous Ideologies with the Wesleyan Way* (Nashville: Abingdon Press, 2019), 24–25, where I also retell this story. This chapter depends heavily upon this earlier work, especially chapter 2, "Joy and the Practice of Hospitality," 21–38.

3. "The Rich Ways of Benedictine Life at Mount Angel," https://www.mountangelabbey.org/monastery/mai/, accessed March 27, 2023.

4. Henri J. M. Nouwen, *Reaching Out: The Three Movements of the Spiritual Life* (New York: Doubleday & Co., 1975), 46.

A Benedictine Wesleyan way takes notice of the centrality of the practice of hospitality in the scriptural witness. It acknowledges that the ability to welcome others begins with a transformed heart of love, peace, and acceptance. It engages in radical action to make room for "the other" as Christ in our midst.

The Practice of Hospitality in Scripture

God's commands about the care of strangers, the neglected and rejected of society, pervade the scriptural witness. The Torah (the first five books of the Bible) brim with hospitality stories. In Genesis, Abraham and Sarah welcome three strangers into their home (Gen 18:1-15). This action, claims Demetrius Dumm, "expressed their readiness to make room for God's mysterious plan in their lives."[5] "You shall also love the stranger," admonishes the ancient historian, "for you were strangers in the land of Egypt" (Deut 10:19). The book of Leviticus contains clear statements about hospitality. "The alien who resides with you shall be to you as the native-born among you; you shall love the alien as yourself, for you were aliens in the land of Egypt" (Lev 19:34). Note how the empathetic response of the faithful depends in some measure on the way in which they have experienced alienation and oppression themselves. True worship, claims the prophet, means "to share your bread with the hungry and bring the homeless poor into your house" (Isa 58:7). In all these cases, joy characterizes the lives of those who offer hospitality to others.

In the Gospels, Christ challenges the narrow definitions of hospitality in his own time. He makes room for those with whom most would never have sought any kind of connection, let alone a relationship. Instead of avoiding the "other," Jesus makes those "others" his friends and companions. He uses those relationships to illustrate the character of his way. All this comes to something of a climax in a parable recorded in the Gospel of Matthew—the judgment of the nations (Matt 25:31-46):

> "Then the king will say to those at his right hand, 'Come, you who are blessed by my Father, inherit the kingdom prepared for you from

---

5. Dumm, *Cherish Christ Above All*, 98.

the foundation of the world, for I was hungry and you gave me food, I was thirsty and you gave me something to drink, I was a stranger and you welcomed me, I was naked and you gave me clothing, I was sick and you took care of me, I was in prison and you visited me.' Then the righteous will answer him, 'Lord, when was it that we saw you hungry and gave you food or thirsty and gave you something to drink? And when was it that we saw you a stranger and welcomed you or naked and gave you clothing? And when was it that we saw you sick or in prison and visited you?' And the king will answer them, 'Truly I tell you, just as you did it to one of the least of these brothers and sisters of mine, you did it to me." (34-40)

Christine Pohl, in her study of the practice of hospitality, *Making Room*, describes the significance of this singular text:

This has been the most important passage for the entire tradition on Christian hospitality. "I was a stranger and you welcomed me" resounds throughout the ancient texts, and contemporary practitioners of hospitality refer to this text more often than to any other passage. Acts of welcoming the stranger, or leaving someone outside cold and hungry, take on intensely heightened significance when it is Jesus himself who experiences the consequences of our ministry or the lack of it.[6]

The remainder of the New Testament reiterates this theme repeatedly. "Do not neglect to show hospitality to strangers," admonishes the writer to the Hebrews, "for by doing that some have entertained angels without knowing it" (13:1-2). In *Ancient Paths*, Benedictine oblate David Robinson explores "The Path of Hospitality" in relation to this pervasive mandate of Scripture. "The God of all creation," he concludes, "invites us to reach out to this world with hospitable hearts, welcoming the poor, the stranger, the homeless, the sick, and the outcast in Jesus' name."[7]

---

6. Christine D. Pohl, *Making Room: Recovering Hospitality as a Christian Tradition* (Grand Rapids: Wm. B. Eerdmans, 1999), 22.

7. David Robinson, *Ancient Paths: Discover Christian Formation the Benedictine Way* (Brewster, MA: Paraclete Press, 2010), 120.

The Hospitable Heart—A Welcoming Attitude

My immersion in the Benedictine and Wesleyan ways has helped me more fully appreciate the wide embrace of these traditions. It has enabled me to conceive hospitality as both attitude and action. I want to explore both dimensions with you, beginning first with the welcoming attitude of someone with a hospitable heart. A collect drawn from the Anglican Service of Morning Prayer, with roots sunk deep in Benedictine spiritualty, continues to shape my thinking about the Christian life and the mandate to follow in the way of Jesus.

> Lord Jesus Christ, you stretched out your arms of love on the hard wood of the cross that everyone might come within the reach of your saving embrace: So clothe us in your Spirit that we, reaching forth our hands in love, may bring those who do not know you to the knowledge and love of you; for the honor of your Name. Amen.[8]

This prayer celebrates the God of wide embrace. I love the image of a God who reaches out and offers that kind of welcome. But the prayer reminds us, as well, that we are called to imitate this God we know in Christ. As ambassadors of reconciliation, we have a ministry of reaching out, welcoming, and embracing. This, in fact, is one of the main ways in which the world comes to know this God of love—through us. The attitude of our heart determines if and how wide we offer our arms of welcome to others.

We say, and rightfully so, that "we love because he first loved us" (1 John 4:19). We can confess with equal fervor that we welcome others because God first welcomed us. God has enveloped us in a loving embrace, so we open our arms to others in the same way. In a fascinating twist of this idea, Benedict locates the roots of our hospitality in the way we offer space to God in our lives. It is a kind of reverse or reciprocal hospitality. He designed the whole monastic life, in fact, as a means of making room for God. Times of prayer are set aside regularly each day to welcome God into our inner sanctum. Psalms are sung

---

8. *Book of Common Prayer* (New York: Church Publishing Inc., 1979), 101.

slowly and intently to expand that space for God's presence and power. Demetrius Dumm puts this so eloquently:

> This radical hospitality, by which the monastic community gladly entertains the divine presence, becomes then the basis for all other forms of hospitality. Those who show reverence and respect for God's mysterious presence among them will also be prepared to honor and respect the share of divine mystery that is found in each and every member of the community.[9]

God opens God's heart to each of us. We offer God hospitality in the citadel of our hearts. This attitude of hospitality translates into a loving welcome for all.

Benedict devotes the entirety of a chapter in his Rule to the practice of hospitality (RB 53) and provides specific instructions for the porter with regards to welcoming guests to the community (RB 66). Much of what he has to say relates to the heart of those who extend this welcome. In his directions "On the Reception of Guests," Benedict lays the theological foundation for an attitude of hospitality no less than three times. "All guests who arrive should be received as Christ" (RB 53:1). "Christ is to be adored in them as it is he who is in fact being received" (7). The greatest care is afforded the poor and travelers "because Christ is received more specially in them" (15). Little wonder that Benedictine writers often describe hospitality as their fourth vow. It reflects the attitude of the heart formed by a divine welcome and shaped in such a way to welcome all as if they were Christ himself. Sister Joan calls this the "recklessly generous heart."[10]

Kathleen Norris makes the point that Benedict places his chapter on hospitality late in the Rule (RB 53) after he has defined the character of the monastic community.[11] Citations from that chapter really stand on their own and require little explanation:

---

9. Dumm, *Cherish Christ Above All*, 122–23.

10. Chittister, *Wisdom Distilled*, 132.

11. See Kathleen Norris, "Hospitality," in Barry, *Wisdom from the Monastery*, 125–27; cf. Tomaine, "Welcoming as Christ: Benedictine Hospitality," in *The Rule of Benedict*, 251–63.

As soon as guests are announced, the superior and the community should hurry to meet them with every mark of love. They should first pray together and thus be united in peace (3-4).

All humility should be shown to the guests on arrival or departure by bowing the head or prostrating the whole body on the ground (6-7).

The superior should pour water on the guest's hands and both the superior and the whole community should wash the feet of all guests (12-13).

The house of God [the guest's quarters] should be in the care of the wise who will manage it wisely (22).

I will never forget reading this chapter for the first time. What impressed me most was how Benedict instructs the superior, for the sake of hospitality, to lay aside important monastic regulations he has just painstakingly laid down. One simple statement speaks volumes. "The superior may break the fast for the sake of guests" (RB 53.10). In order to honor Christ, silence is broken, a table is set, and the superior breaks bread with the guest. We see the same qualities exemplified in the porter who serves as the first line of hospitality for visitors and strangers. Benedict instructs:

Let a wise old person be placed at the door of the monastery. . . . As soon as anyone knocks or a poor person calls out, the porter answers, "Thanks be to God" or "Your blessing, please," and, with all the gentleness of the fear of God, promptly answers with the warmth of love. (RB 66.1, 3-4)

"Thank God you are here." Through this portrait of the porter, Benedict gives us a vision of how to live with an open and loving heart. Like the porter, as Jane Tomaine claims, "we can be *available, attentive, and accepting*."[12]

The Wesleys conceived a heart of hospitality in their own day

---

12. Tomaine, *The Rule of Benedict*, 262.

primarily in terms of generous inclusivity.[13] A strongly elitist system characterized British society—a world in which everyone was expected to stay in their place. Seismic changes, however, were already beginning to tear apart the fabric of society on the eve of the industrial revolution. Thousands were migrating from the countryside into burgeoning urban centers. These masses of the poor were seldom welcomed with open arms. The Methodist Societies established a reputation, however, with regard to their wide embrace. Charles Wesley developed some of his most powerful hymns around this theme, many of them having to do with the expansion of the heart toward others. The Methodists, especially the women, sang them and lived them with fervor.

The heart, emptied of a preoccupation with self, finds room for the ever-expanding love of Christ that can then be offered to others. "Filled with purity of love," one young woman of whom Wesley sang, embraced the world with wide-spread arms:

> Celestial charity expands
> > Her heart to all the human race;
> Though knit to Christ in closest bands,
> > Her soul doth every soul embrace.
> She no unkind exception makes,
> > A childlike follower of her God;
> The world into her heart she takes,
> > The purchase dear of Jesu's blood.[14]

Another explicitly sought to discern the face of Christ in all she met. This practice shaped her into a person whose love led her to embrace the whole world:

> Nursing the poor with constant care,
> > Affection soft, and heart-esteem,
> She saw her Savior's image there,
> > And gladly ministered to Him.[15]

---

13. See the section on "Generous Inclusivity" in Paul W. Chilcote, "Charles Wesley and Christian Practices," *Proceedings of The Charles Wesley Society* 12 (2008): 35–47.

14. Wesley, MS Funeral Hymns, 45.

15. Wesley, MS Funeral Hymns, 51–53.

Struggling to find the right words to express the hospitality of the heart, Charles created this magnificent image of the one who stretched out her arms of love, "*ingrasping* all mankind."[16]

Radical Hospitality—Love in Action

You can sense, I am sure, how this attitude of welcome moves seamlessly into hospitable action. And this action has power—the power of love. In her acclaimed memoir, *The Cloister Walk*, Kathleen Norris describes the way in which acts of hospitality she experienced in Benedictine communities opened the doors of her heart to the Christian faith.[17] Actions speak louder than words. The act of welcoming others proclaims a message of love and acceptance into a world characterized by forces that push us apart. Radical hospitality, or love in action in the world, changes lives. "Benedict's vision of hospitality," writes David Robinson, "is a radical call to transform society, person by person, through spiritual and physical means, as it seeks to welcome Christ through the stranger, the sick, the homeless, and the poor by working to provide for the needy in the community and praying for the needy around the world."[18] Wesleyans share this goal. My own United Methodist Church explicitly seeks "to make disciples of Jesus Christ for the transformation of the world."[19] Acts of radical hospitality move us closer to this goal.

A story from the journal of an early Methodist woman demonstrates her deep desire for her heart and her actions to be in sync. It illustrates the Wesleyan principle of a hospitable heart extended into the world through action—heart and hands held together:

> I am ashamed and confounded before God for what has happened this day. A woman with three children came to my door to ask for charity. I found my heart rise against her; but why, I could give no reason. I did relieve her, but I am sure much against my mind. *This*

---

16. Wesley, *MS Funeral Hymns*, 56.

17. See Kathleen Norris, *The Cloister Walk* (New York: Riverhead Books, 1996).

18. Robinson, *Ancient Paths*, 121.

19. *The Book of Discipline of The United Methodist Church* (Nashville: The United Methodist Publishing House, 2016), ¶120.

cannot be loving. But whatever it was, it drove me to God both for myself and the woman and her children. I am ashamed before God for the unchristian temper I felt in myself. Amen![20]

She yearned for a life of action flowing from a heart filled with welcoming love. But note, in this particular instance, how her actions helped get her heart in the right place. Her actions helped open her heart to be able to share her whole self with someone in need.

Sister Joan made the same kind of spiritual discovery about her community's rule of life: "I discovered you see," she confesses, "that real Benedictinism requires us to pour ourselves out for the other, to give ourselves away, to provide the staples of life, both material and spiritual for one another. . . . That's what hospitality is all about. Not abundance and not totality. Just sharing. Real sharing."[21] Over the years I have returned again and again to Basil Pennington's lesson from the monastery titled "Welcome Again."[22] His lessons about welcoming, sharing, and growing spiritually have been invaluable: (1) Hospitality is not an abstract principle, it is a down-to-earth, habituated practice. (2) We tell how well God's means of grace are shaping our lives by how faithfully we are living in solidarity with Christ in the poor. (3) A life of hospitality is not easy; it requires patience, imagination, and good humor. (4) We learn how to love through the ordinary practice of loving others by welcoming them into our lives wholeheartedly.

Healing takes place whenever we make room in our lives for others in this way, and particularly for those in need. And this healing flows in both directions, both to the one invited in and to the one who welcomes. Hospitality has to do with creating safe space for others, and whenever we have the courage to make room we enter into the sacred space of faithful love. An early Methodist discovered this through an intuition that led to action:

20. Paul W. Chilcote, *Her Own Story: Autobiographical Portraits of Early Methodist Women* (Nashville: Kingswood Books, 2001), 74.

21. Chittister, *Wisdom Distilled*, 123.

22. Pennington, *Lessons from the Monastery*, 49–51.

One forenoon, having taken a walk to visit some of the people, I passed a house where a child was crying most pitifully. I stopped a moment to listen, and then went into the house. I said to the mother, "What is the matter with your child?" The poor woman, with tears in her eyes, said, "I have little or no milk, and believe it is crying for hunger." I said, "Let me give it some milk," which the child took with great eagerness. I then requested her to bring it to our house every day, at a certain time, which she did. In about a fortnight it was so much altered that her husband said, "The preaching woman has cured my child. I will go to hear her; perhaps she will cure my soul." He came and got awakened. His wife also. And they both united with us in class and soon found peace with God. O may I meet them in heaven![23]

It should be no surprise, therefore, that the Wesleyan ministry of hospitality became a mission lived out in solidarity with those people who were shut out, neglected, and thrown away. Charles in his hymns and John in his preaching both admonished their followers to "make the poor their friends." And they sang their way into the hearts and lives of these companions—those with whom they literally "shared their bread" (the actual meaning of the word):

> The poor as Jesus' bosom-friends,
>> the poor he makes his latest care,
> to all his followers commends,
>> and wills us on our hands to bear;
> the poor our dearest care we make,
>> and love them for our Savior's sake.

In my discussion of community in chapter 2 I introduced you to Mary Bosanquet and her neo-monastic family in Leytonstone, a noteworthy ministry of hospitality in a poor and depressed area of London.[24] She intended to provide a home for the most destitute. She created a small community of women who cared for the poor, neglected, and marginalized neighbors she had befriended there. Over

---

23. Chilcote, *Her Own Story*, 169.
24. See Paul W. Chilcote, "An Early Methodist Community of Women," *Methodist History* 38, no. 4 (July 2000): 219–30.

the course of five years they sheltered and cared for thirty-five children and thirty-four women. John Wesley described their "experiment" as one of the most exemplary developments within his movement. All accounts emphasize the fact that the primary characteristic of this community was joy. A Benedictine Wesleyan way puts hospitality at the very center of life together and thereby discovers the inexpressible sweetness of love.

Let us not forget that each of us has opportunity every day to meet Christ in the face of our children, partners, neighbors, and strangers, and to open our arms to these people in love. When some groups in the United States were stoking up fear against Muslims, my daughter, Anna, felt compelled to do something. She had seen a young Muslim woman regularly at the gym and approached her after a workout one day. "I just wanted to see how you're doing with everything that's happening in the world today," she said. "I'm sure it's got to be hard and I just want you to know you're not alone. I'm standing with you." She burst into tears and they hugged for a while. This stranger felt welcomed, safe, and loved. Together, they took a leap of faith. They decided to bring their Muslim and Christian friends together—to provide a safe space for conversation and connection. A simple act of kindness and hospitality launched a deep friendship that blossomed into a place of healing.

Abraham and Sarah invited in three strangers to share a meal. The Bakers provided a chair at their Sunday dinner table for a lonely prisoner. A monastic superior shares food with a guest in the community. Jesus invites us to his table and opens his arms wide. Charles Wesley sings, "Let every soul be Jesus' guest, / You need not one be left behind. . . . The invitation is to all. . . . In Christ a hearty welcome find."[25] Who do we see in the face of the guest? As a conclusion to her discussion of hospitality in the Rule, Esther de Waal leaves us with two simple questions to ponder about the guest and about ourselves: "Did we see Christ in them? Did they see Christ in us?"[26]

* * *

---

25. Wesley, *Redemption Hymns*, 63–66.
26. de Waal, *Seeking God*, 121.

A Biblical Treasure

The parable of the judgment of the nations includes that all-important phrase, "I was a stranger and you welcomed me." But the whole story exudes the welcoming spirit of Christ.

> "Then the king will say to those at his right hand, 'Come, you that are blessed by my Father, inherit the kingdom prepared for you from the foundation of the world; for I was hungry and you gave me food, I was thirsty and you gave me something to drink, I was a stranger and you welcomed me, I was naked and you gave me clothing, I was sick and you took care of me, I was in prison and you visited me.' Then the righteous will answer him, 'Lord, when was it that we saw you hungry and gave you food or thirsty and gave you something to drink? And when was it that we saw you a stranger and welcomed you, or naked and gave you clothing? And when was it that we saw you sick or in prison and visited you?' And the king will answer them, 'Truly I tell you, just as you did it to one of the least of these brothers and sisters of mine, you did it to me.'" (Matt 25:34-40)

A Benedictine Treasure

Collects play a major role in the Anglican tradition of daily prayer, shaped by the opus Dei of the Benedictine tradition. This collect for Mission figures prominently in the Service of Morning Prayer.

> Lord Jesus Christ, you stretched out your arms of love on the hard wood
> of the cross
> that everyone might come within the reach of your saving embrace:
> So clothe us in your Spirit that we, reaching forth our hands in love,
> may bring those who do not know you to the knowledge and love of you;
> for the honor of your Name. Amen.[27]

A Wesleyan Treasure

Charles Wesley wrote many eucharistic hymns based on meal stories in the New Testament. This lyrical paraphrase of the parable of the

---

27. *Book of Common Prayer* (1979), 101.

great dinner (Luke 14:15-24) celebrates God's welcome of all to the table.

> Come, sinners, to the gospel feast,
> Let every soul be Jesus' guest,
> You need not one be left behind,
> For God hath bid all humankind.
>
> Sent by my Lord, on you I call,
> The invitation is to all.
> Come, all the world! Come, sinner, thou!
> All things in Christ are ready now.
>
> Come, all ye souls by sin oppressed,
> Ye restless wanderers after rest;
> Ye poor, and maimed, and halt, and blind,
> In Christ a hearty welcome find.[28]

---

28. Wesley, *Redemption Hymns*, 63–66.

Chapter 9

Holiness

Be perfect, therefore, as your heavenly Father is perfect. —Matthew 5:48
Be holy that you may more truly be called so. —Benedict
The recovery of the image of God is the one thing needful. —Charles Wesley

In my journey of faith, I have often turned to the words of Francis de Sales for encouragement:

> There are many who want me to tell them of secret ways of becoming perfect and I can only tell them that the sole secret is a hearty love of God, and the only way of attaining that love is by loving. You learn to speak by speaking, to study by studying, to run by running, to work by working; and just so you learn to love God and [neighbor] by loving. Begin as a mere apprentice and the very power of love will lead you on to become a master of the art.[1]

I want this final chapter to feel more like an invitation to love than a discussion of holiness. I hope that you are captured by the inspiring vision of love for God and love for everything else in God that Benedict and the Wesleys shared. I pray that you will join me and so many others as an apprentice to love under the instruction of Christ. In a Benedictine Wesleyan way, holiness means to "let the same mind be in you that was in Christ Jesus" (Phil 2:5)—to be "conformed to the image of [Christ]" (Rom 8:29). This final common goal is a personal and a cosmic vision of restoration in which

---

1. Francis de Sales, *The Secret of Sanctity*, trans. Ella McMahon (New York: Benziger, 1893), 256.

everyone can participate. Holiness means to become, like Christ, a master in the art of love.

Dallas Willard, in our own time, reclaimed the imagery of apprenticeship with regards to our journey with Christ. While neither of the Wesleys nor Benedict ever used this kind of language, it resonates well with their vision of life in Christ. In works such as *The Divine Conspiracy*, *The Great Omission*, and *Renovation of the Heart*, Willard claims that God's primary intention is for everyone to become a Christlike child. He describes spiritual transformation into Christlikeness as "the process of forming the inner world of the human self in such a way that it takes on the character of the inner being of Jesus himself."[2] To become holy, essentially, means to become truly and fully human—to become real—to resemble Christ in every way.

The quest for Christian perfection and the goal of perfect love defined the lives of John and Charles Wesley. They taught that the Spirit conforms the believer more and more to Christ through a process of sanctification, or growth in grace. They emphasized twin dimensions in this process: holiness of heart (internal holiness) or love of God (a vertical dimension) and holiness of life (external holiness) or love of neighbor (a horizontal dimension). They sought to love God deeply, but they also embraced God's relational way of love in the world. They longed for God's new creation—both the restoration of their hearts and the renovation of the world. They affirmed that all Christians can grow into the perfect love God has promised in Christ. But this entails a lengthy process of cooperation with the Spirit and never-ending reliance on Christ. To put it simply, they believed holiness equals happiness. Perfection, holiness, entire sanctification, perfect love were simply so many terms to denote one thing—loving God above all else and all else in God.

My first serious introduction to the Benedictine tradition was the joint conference with Methodists on the theme of sanctification that I described in the preface. It was a deep dive into this large topic. I

---

2. Dallas Willard, *Renovation of the Heart: Putting on the Character of Christ* (Colorado Springs: NavPress, 2002), 159; cf. his works *The Divine Conspiracy: Rediscovering Our Hidden Life in God* (San Francisco: HarperSanFrancisco, 1998); and *The Great Omission: Reclaiming Jesus's Essential Teachings on Discipleship* (New York: HarperOne, 2006).

remember many of the Benedictine presenters stressing the point that Benedict's way was not just for monks or nuns, but for all Christians, and that the "heights of perfection" were possible in this life.[3] Paschal Cheline of Mount Angel Abbey—later to become a dear friend—was asked to provide something of a summative statement about the Rule as a practical guide to holiness:

> Benedict's program is not for an elitist group within the Christian body, but rather for ordinary people. On this general level we find a true common ground between Benedict and John Wesley. The desire to build a plan, to offer a program, that leads the ordinary person to holiness—this was, it seems to me, in the heart of each of these men.[4]

In a brilliant address, Terence Kardong identified five key elements in a Benedictine understanding of perfection:

(1) The primary objective of perfection is not flawlessness; it is love.
(2) Perfection is not static; it is dynamic.
(3) God intends this experience for everyone; perfect love is not an elitist quest.
(4) Justice for the community is as important as individual communion with God.
(5) Perfection is not really an achievement; it is a gift of grace.[5]

The following statements characterize John and Charles Wesley's areas of agreement with regard to their own vision:

(1) *Love.* Christian perfection is the fullest possible love of God and neighbor.
(2) *Purity of Intention.* Perfection is seeking to please God singularly in all things.

3. See statements by Jerome Theisen, Terence G. Kardong, and Paschal G. Cheline, all in *Sanctification in the Benedictine and Wesleyan Traditions*, 11, 46, and 328, respectively.

4. Paschal G. Cheline, "Holiness of Heart and Mind: A Benedictine Perspective," in *Sanctification in the Benedictine and Wesleyan Traditions*, 328.

5. Terence G. Kardong, "Benedict's Puzzling Theme of Perfection," in *Sanctification in the Benedictine and Wesleyan Traditions*, 49–50.

(3) *Dynamism.* Perfection in the Christian life is dynamic, not static, in nature.

(4) *Restoration.* Perfection is the fullest possible restoration of God's image.

(5) *Happiness.* Perfection is happiness—a "blessed abiding" in God.[6]

These statements are extremely helpful, especially for those of us who feel like novices in this great quest. They instill in me, at least, a sense of hope. But, truth to be told, the Wesleys and Benedict were practical theologians. Their primary interest lay in the saints whose lives illustrate the triumph of love in life. As practitioners of love, they were inspired when they saw lofty principles about love lived out faithfully and effectively in the practicalities of "real life." Concrete examples show us that love is real and can be lived out day by day in relationship with God and others. The stories of faithful, holy people invite us into the quest for perfect love, and no one is excluded from this path.

Benedict goes so far as to say that the holy ones can lead you "to the very heights of perfection" (RB 73.2). Beyond the holy exemplars within Scripture, he alludes in the Rule to the inspirational lives of Basil of Caesarea and Cassian (RB 73.4-5). Basil was known for his love of the poor and his care for the underprivileged, as well as for establishing guidelines for monastic life. Cassian possessed a deep wisdom that love formed in his soul. Most certainly Athanasius's *Life of St. Antony* shaped Benedict's own vision, as well as the lives of a cloud of monastic witnesses including Pachomius, Ambrose, and Augustine among many others.

Between 1749 and 1755 John Wesley collected Christian biographical and devotional material into *A Christian Library* of fifty volumes![7] Clement of Alexandria's portrait of the perfect Christian provided John Wesley's model for the character of a Methodist. The lives of two Catholic

---

6. Adapted from Paul W. Chilcote, "Spirituality in the Wesleyan Tradition," in *The Quest for Love Divine: Select Essays in Wesleyan Theology and Practice* (Eugene, OR: Cascade Books, 2022), 183. For a fuller exposition, see my introduction to John Wesley's Christian perfection corpus in John Wesley, *The Works of John Wesley*, vol. 13, *Doctrinal and Controversial Treatises II*, ed. Paul W. Chilcote and Kenneth J. Collins (Nashville: Abingdon Press, 2013), 3–25.

7. John Wesley, *A Christian Library*, 50 vols. (Bristol: Felix Farley, 1749–55).

figures—Gregory Lopez and Gaston de Renty—particularly influenced his vision of holiness or perfection. He grouped them together with Thomas à Kempis as examples of "real, inward Christians."[8] A Benedictine Wesleyan way affirms that these examples of "lived love" inspire us all and can expand our hearts to love more fully. Benedict and the Wesleys believed in the power and possibility of love. They saw holiness or "perfect love" in others and sought to emulate it.

The parallels between Benedict and the Wesleys are just so striking with regards to their vision of holiness. Their reflections on this essential goal of the Christian life, from their own perspectives in their own times, converge in three salient themes. First, they conceive holiness as an ongoing process of spiritual growth—the restoration of the image of Christ (*imago Christi*). Second, they cannot understand holiness apart from life together and the experience of God's beloved community—the peaceable reign of Christ. Third, ultimately holiness means the fullest possible love of God and the fullest possible love of all else in God.

The Restoration of the Image of God

In one of his most significant sermons, Charles Wesley defines "The One Thing Needful" as the "restoration of the image of God."

> The recovery of the image of God, of glorious liberty, of this perfect soundness, is the one thing needful upon earth. This appears first from the fact that the enjoyment of perfect freedom and health was the singular purpose of our creation. For to this end you were created, to love God; and to this end alone, even to love the Lord your God with all your heart, soul, mind, and strength. But love is the very image of God. It is the brightness of God's glory. By love you are not only made like God, but in some sense one with God.[9]

Both brothers viewed redemption as a process of divine therapy (*therapeia*)—healing or restoration. In his reflections on the preface

---

8. See Wesley, *Works*, 2:374–75. I have already reviewed the influence of à Kempis with regards to "humility" above.

9. Kenneth G. C. Newport, ed., *The Sermons of Charles Wesley* (Oxford: Oxford University Press, 2001), 365.

of Benedict's Rule, Columba Cary-Elwes reveals a deeper meaning in Benedict's words, "having opened our eyes to the divine light [*deificum lumen*], let us hear with attentive ears what the divine voice cries out to us daily" (RB Prol.9). "The word is stronger than 'divine,'" Cary-Elwes maintains. "It means 'divinizing,' that is, 'making Godlike.'"[10] A Benedictine Wesleyan way invites everyone into a process of spiritual growth by which God restores the image of Christ—the capacity to love as Christ loves.

To put this simply, Benedict built his Rule and the Wesleys their program of discipleship on the assumption that real growth in love is possible in life. They were not satisfied with being forgiven sinners only; they longed to be loving children of God. Their optimism in the power of God's grace stands in stark contrast to the many forms of pessimism about people in our world. This confidence in the Holy Spirit's work in our lives provides hope for the average person. Restoration begins with the heart, any person's heart. "Write thy new name upon my heart," sings Charles, "Thy new, best name of Love."[11] But God's process of restoration engages every facet of who we are until we become transparent to the Love who recreates us. Charles sets the goal:

> Finish then thy new creation,
>> Pure and spotless let us be,
> Let us see thy great salvation,
>> Perfectly restored in thee;
> Changed from glory into glory,
>> Till in heaven we take our place,
> Till we cast our crowns before thee,
>> Lost in wonder, love, and praise![12]

In a Benedictine Wesleyan way, to have the image of God restored means to become Christlike. Benedict expresses his aspirations for all monastics in very practical terms:

---

10. Columba Cary-Elwes, "Letter and Spirit: St. Benedict's Rule for Our Times," *The Way* 40 (1981 Supplement): 15, https://www.theway.org.uk/Back/s040Elwes1.pdf, accessed May 21, 2023.

11. Wesley, *Hymns and Sacred Poems* (1742), 30–31.

12. Wesley, *Redemption Hymns*, 12.

Your way of acting should be different from the world's way. Prefer nothing to the love of Christ. You are not to act in anger or nurse a grudge. Rid your heart of all deceit. Never give a false greeting of peace or turn away from charity to another. . . . Love your enemies. Do not curse those who curse you, but bless them instead. . . . Do not desire to be called holy before you really are, but be holy first, that you may truly be called so. Fulfill God's commands in your actions every day. . . . Respect the elders and love the young. Pray for your enemies out of love of Christ. . . . "Eye has not seen, nor ear heard, what is prepared for those who love God." (RB 4.20-26, 31-32, 62-63, 70-72, 77)

In one of his hymns on the Trinity, Charles uses poetic language to express the way in which God's process of restoration empties and then fills the soul. The Spirit consumes, blots out, erases, and drives out sins, removing all barriers that separate us from God. The Spirit floods, fills, immerses, imparts, restores—teaches us to love:

> And when we rise in love renewed,
> Our souls resemble thee,
> An image of the Triune God
>   To all eternity.[13]

In his sermon "Patience," John provides a portrait of those in whom love is restored:

> They increase in love, lowliness, meekness, in every part of the image of God . . . continual love bringing continual joy in the Lord, they rejoice evermore. They converse continually with the God whom they love, unto whom in everything they give thanks. And as they now love God with all their heart and with all their soul and with all their mind and with all their strength, so Jesus now reigns alone in their heart, the Lord of every motion there.[14]

---

13. Charles Wesley, *Hymns on the Trinity* (Bristol: Pine, 1767), 58.
14. Wesley, *Works*, 3:175–76.

The Peaceable Reign of Christ

Benedict and the Wesleys were not only interested in changed lives. They wanted to change the world. They believed the way to do this was to create communities of peace in which the love of God shaped every dimension of life together. Like many of the fresh expressions of church in our time, their hope was that this love inside the community would radiate out into the world. They believed in the infectious nature of love. They wanted it to spread as rapidly as we have seen viruses move across our globe. They had a Revelation 11:15 vision: "The kingdom of the world has become the kingdom of our Lord and of his Messiah, and he will reign forever and ever." I hope that gets your blood pumping!

What did the love of God compel them to do? It compelled Benedict to open his doors to anyone who came knocking. It compelled John Wesley to write his very last letter to encourage William Wilberforce to continue his abolitionist work. It led a Benedictine oblate, Dorothy Day, to open her heart and her home to the most destitute. It led Methodists like Frank Mason North to launch a campaign against child labor and to recapture the vision of a "social gospel." He concludes his most famous hymn with this renewed vision of life:

> Till all the world shall learn your love
> and follow where your feet have trod,
> till, glorious from your heaven above,
> shall come the city of our God![15]

The biblical vision of God's "beloved community" was the central principle of the thought and activity of Martin Luther King Jr.[16] Walter Brueggemann used the Hebrew word *shalom* to describe "a caring, sharing, rejoicing community with none to make them afraid."[17] Charles

---

15. Quoted in Paul W. Chilcote, *Singing the Faith: Soundings of Lyrical Theology in the Methodist Tradition* (Nashville: Wesley's Foundery Books, 2020), 92.
16. Kenneth L. Smith and Ira G. Zepp Jr., *Search for the Beloved Community: The Thinking of Martin Luther King, Jr.* (Valley Forge: Judson Press, 1974), 119–40.
17. Walter Brueggemann, *Living Toward a Vision: Biblical Reflections on Shalom* (Cleveland: United Church Press, 1976), 20.

Wesley developed his own language to paint a compelling portrait of God's rule in the world.[18] He describes God's kingdom as a "quiet and peaceable reign."

> Come then to thy servants again,
>> Who long thy appearing to know,
> Thy quiet and peaceable reign
>> In mercy establish below:
> All sorrow before thee shall fly,
>> And anger and hatred be o'er,
> And envy and malice shall die,
>> And discord afflict us no more.

He concludes this prayer to Christ with an expression of hope for a world in which we "kindly each other embrace, / And love with a passion like thine."[19]

A Benedictine Wesleyan way understands holiness as life together in God's beloved community—the peaceable reign of Christ that has the power to transform the world. "Benedict's vision of the peaceable kingdom was a real one," writes Sister Joan. "Benedict sketched out a blueprint for world peace."[20] She views the entire Rule—the monastic life he designed—as a path leading to peace in community.[21] I have often returned to Sister Joan's reflections on peace in *Wisdom Distilled from the Daily*. I know of no more profound exposition of Benedict's vision of the kingdom. She writes:

> Real Benedictine peace comes from living the Paschal mystery well, from being willing to die to things that keep us from the fullness of life, from confronting culture with the memory of the cross, from

---

18. See Paul W. Chilcote, *A Faith That Sings: Biblical Themes in the Lyrical Theology of Charles Wesley* (Eugene, OR: Cascade Books, 2017), 106–21. Many of the insights presented here depend greatly upon this earlier work.

19. Charles Wesley, *Hymns for the Nativity of Our Lord* (London: Strahan, 1745), 23–24.

20. Chittister, *The Monastery of the Heart*, 127.

21. See Terence Kardong, "Benedict's Peaceable Kingdom," *Benedictines* 21, no. 1 (1966): 17–26, where he demonstrates the centrality of justice in Benedict's understanding of the kingdom of God.

letting nothing deter us from the will of God in life, from living immersed in Christ to such a degree that eventually nothing else matters and witness becomes an imperative. . . . Monastic peace, in other words, is the power to face what is with the serenity of faith and the courage of hope, with the surety that good can come from evil and the certainty that good will triumph. . . . Benedictine spirituality brings this model of peace-through-justice to every place it builds and breathes.[22]

I'll never forget the first time I saw Desmond Tutu in person. It was at the World Methodist Conference held in Nairobi in 1986, nearly a decade before the fall of the racist system of apartheid in South Africa. I can still see him waving a Bible over his head and proclaiming, "Apartheid is dead! Apartheid is dead!" He had learned from the Bible and Martin Luther King Jr. that the arch of the moral universe is long, but it always bends toward justice. He knew that peace was just around the corner. This is the hard work of love. John Wesley believed God raised up the people called Methodists not only for the purpose of proclaiming personal holiness but also to spread scriptural holiness—the peaceable reign of Christ—throughout the world. We are invited to continue in this labor of love.

Love of God and Love of Neighbor

In a single-stanza hymn, Charles Wesley reflects on the ultimate meaning of holiness—on the ultimate meaning of life:

> God wills that I should holy be;
> > That holiness I long to feel,
> That full divine conformity
> > To all my Savior's righteous will.
> See, Lord, the travail of your soul
> > Accomplished in the change of mine,
> And plunge me, every whit made whole,
> > In all the depths of love divine.[23]

---

22. Chittister, *Wisdom Distilled*, 183, 184–85, 191.
23. Wesley, 324.

He claims that God deeply desires for everyone to become loving, to be holy. All God's children exist for this very purpose. He infers that all people have a deep longing for this as well, whether they acknowledge it or not. In the end, God's love is a mystery into which we plunge ourselves.

The golden thread that runs through Benedict's Rule is the "thread of love—love of God and love of one another," wrote Father Paschal. "His Rule is a call to love and is a sure way for one to learn to live in love."[24] "First of all," Benedict instructs, "love God with your whole heart, your whole soul, and all your strength, and love your neighbor as yourself" (RB 4.1). Like Benedict, when John Wesley was pressed to define his vision of the holy life, he simply says:

> It is the "loving the Lord his God with all his heart, and with all his soul, and with all his mind." This is the sum of Christian perfection. It is all comprised in that one word, love. The first branch of it is the love of God, and as they that love God love their brothers and sisters also, it is inseparably connected with the second, "Thou shalt love thy neighbor as thyself." You shall love everyone as your own soul, as Christ loved us.[25]

Benedict speaks of our "walking" in this path only once. In all other references, it is all about running! His words at the close of the prologue continue to inspire me to this day: "As we advance in this way of life and in faith, we shall run the way of God's commandments with expanded hearts overflowing with the inexpressible sweetness of love" (RB Prol. 49).

Once Charles Wesley had experienced this sweet love, he made the pursuit of this kind of holiness his primary goal. "His subsequent spiritual life," as J. Ernest Rattenbury stated so succinctly, "might be summed up compendiously in one phrase: 'a quest for love.'"[26] Perhaps no words he penned ever expressed his passion about this quest more than these:

---

24. Cheline, "Holiness of Heart and Mind," 335.

25. Wesley, *Works*, 3:74.

26. J. Ernest Rattenbury, *The Evangelical Doctrines of Charles Wesley's Hymns* (London: Epworth, 1941), 278.

To love is all my wish,
I only live for this:
Grant me, Lord, my heart's desire,
There by faith forever dwell:
This I always will require
Thee and only thee to feel.

Thy power I pant to prove
Rooted and fixed in love,
Strengthened by thy Spirit's might,
Wise to fathom things divine,
What the length and breadth and height,
What the depth of love like thine.

Ah! Give me this to know
With all thy saints below.
Swells my soul to compass thee,
Gasps in thee to live and move,
Filled with all the deity,
All immersed and lost in love![27]

As we come to the close of this journey, I want to speak to you directly and passionately. I believe the world desperately needs this vision of a Benedictine Wesleyan way. We need to be invited to move forward toward this common goal of holiness—love of God above all else and all else in God. I have encountered so many versions of the Christian faith that are passive, static, and self-inflated. Instead of filling you up with truth and joy and peace and love, they leave you hungry and thirsty. I long for you to feast on love, to practice love, to become love.

A Benedictine Wesleyan way proclaims that no force in the universe is more powerful than love. Love overcomes hate. Love triumphs over evil. Love can conquer the disobedient heart. Love never coerces. Love never fails. My prayer is that love will fill your soul. My hope is that God's love will fill the soul of every child of God. When this happens, our hearts and our world will be filled with peace, and our joy

---

27. Wesley, *Hymns and Sacred Poems* (1739), 169.

will be beyond our wildest imagination. When we invite God to restore our lives and our world, Christ will be all in all, and praise will reign. Sister Joan beautifully describes the outcome of this "conversion of life" so central to her own heritage and the common goal of a Benedictine Wesleyan way: "all things [will] call us to melt into one great paean of praise for the joy of having found the God we continue to seek."[28]

* * *

A Biblical Treasure

In the Gospel of Matthew, a Pharisee seeks to test Christ by asking him a difficult question. His response—the Great Commandment—articulates his vision of the goal of life for his followers, and indeed, for all those in the human family.

> He said to him, "'You shall love the Lord your God with all your heart and with all your soul and with all your mind.' This is the greatest and first commandment. And a second is like it: 'You shall love your neighbor as yourself.' On these two commandments hang all the Law and the Prophets." (Matt 22:37-40)

A Benedictine Treasure

I first discovered Bernard of Clairvaux through reading his brief treatise *On Love of God*. In this Christmas prayer you sense the profound reality of God's love incarnate in the Holy Child.

> *Let Your goodness Lord appear to us, that we,*
> *made in your image, conform ourselves to it.*
> *In our own strength*
> *we cannot imitate Your majesty, power, and wonder*
> *nor is it fitting for us to try.*
> *But Your mercy reaches from the heavens*
> *through the clouds to the earth below.*

---

28. Chittister, *The Monastery of the Heart*, 98.

You have come to us as a small child,
but you have brought us the greatest of all gifts,
the gift of eternal love
Caress us with Your tiny hands,
embrace us with Your tiny arms
and pierce our hearts with Your soft, sweet cries. Amen.

A Wesleyan Treasure

Love of God and love of neighbor define holiness in a Benedictine Wesleyan way. Charles Wesley sings with passion about being captured by this kind of love. Make this hymn your prayer today:

To love is all my wish,
I only live for this:
Grant me, Lord, my heart's desire,
There by faith forever dwell:
This I always will require
Thee and only thee to feel.

Thy power I pant to prove
Rooted and fixed in love,
Strengthened by thy Spirit's might,
Wise to fathom things divine,
What the length and breadth and height,
What the depth of love like thine.

Ah! Give me this to know
With all thy saints below.
Swells my soul to compass thee,
Gasps in thee to live and move,
Filled with all the deity,
All immersed and lost in love![29]

---

29. Wesley, *Hymns and Sacred Poems* (1739), 169.

Epilogue

I will never forget the day I was invited to join the monks in the choir to sing the Daily Office at Mount Angel Abbey. The invitation surprised me. I had not expected it, nor had I even thought about it as a possibility. In my mind it was a sheer act of hospitality, an open door to join the monks in the way. It scared me half to death. I feared all the mistakes I would make. Would I remember when to stand at the right time? Would I be able to chant the Psalms correctly? Would anyone be watching me as I potentially stumbled through it all? It thrilled me to the depth of my being. I could not wait for the Office to begin. I longed to join my voice with my brothers as part of our life together. The monk by my side put me completely at ease. He guided me through each step of the way. He made me feel like I belonged. God's love overwhelmed me as I sang the songs of praise and prayed the prayers of the community.

This book comes to its close with this epilogue, but your journey really just begins; my journey just begins. All of us are novices as we follow this path to God in companionship—under apprenticeship—with Christ. We all have so much to learn because the way is all about love, and love is like that. No matter how deep we go, there are always greater depths to explore. No matter how high we go, there are always greater heights to experience. The inexpressible sweetness of love knows no bounds. But as is the case with all journeys, the journey of life together does have a beginning, a middle, and an end. This way moves toward a goal. If you find yourself at the beginning, I pray that this book has given you a good foundation upon which to build. If you are somewhere in the middle, I hope that you have embraced new visions of life together, discovered new practices, and are eager to stretch out toward goals rooted in love. If you feel that you are near the journey's end, I encourage you to reach out toward the flying goal of love that Christ lays before you as "the pioneer and perfecter of faith" (Heb 12:2).

The Spirit of Christ is blowing fresh wind into the life of the church today. I am convinced of this. Like every age of renewal or reform, there are signs of saving faith in fresh expressions of church where people are gathering around the living Word. Disciples of Christ are rediscovering the importance of mutual accountability. They are practicing faith in a way that combines deep interiority with active service in the world. Followers of Christ are experiencing the connections between the vital worship of God and their mission in the world. At such a time as this, I believe we need to drop our buckets into the deep wells of Christian wisdom. We have so many lessons to learn from those who have come before us in the pilgrimage of faith. As in the parable of the Sower (Matt 13:1-9), I pray that the new seed being sewn in our time will find its way into the rich soil of time-honored Christian practice. I believe deeply that a Benedictine Wesleyan way provides foundational visions, practices, and goals to sustain us in this recovery and restoration. I hope you have received it here as a gift of the Spirit of Christ.

I think it fitting to close with words from our mentors, John and Charles Wesley and Benedict of Nursia. May they be words of encouragement to you as you pursue a Benedictine Wesleyan way.

> Let *love* not visit you as a transient guest, but be the constant ruling quality of your soul. See that your heart is filled at all times and on all occasions with real, genuine benevolence, not to those only that love *you*, but to every soul. Let it pant in your heart, let it sparkle in your eyes, let it shine in all your actions.[1]
> —John Wesley

---

1. Wesley, *Works*, 3:422–23.

Thy nature, gracious Lord, impart;
Come quickly from above;
Write thy new name upon my heart,
Thy new, best name of Love.[2]
—Charles Wesley

Prefer nothing whatever to Christ,
and may he lead us all together to life everlasting.
(RB 72.11-12)
—Benedict

---

2. Wesley, *Hymns and Sacred Poems* (1742), 30–31.

Bibliographical Index

"An Account of Mrs. Sarah Ryan." *Arminian Magazine* 2 (1779): 296–310.

Athanasius. *The Life of Antony.* Translated by Robert C. Gregg. New York: Paulist Press, 1980.

Baker, Frank. *Methodism and the Love-Feast.* London: Epworth Press, 1957.

Barry, Patrick et al. *Wisdom from the Monastery: The Rule of Benedict for Everyday Life.* Collegeville, MN: Liturgical Press, 2006.

Begbie, Jeremy S. *Music, Modernity, and God: Essays in Listening.* Oxford: Oxford University Press, 2013.

Bennet, William, ed. *Memoirs of Grace Bennet.* Macclesfield: E. Bayley, 1803.

Best, Gary. *Charles Wesley: A Biography.* Peterborough: Epworth Press, 2006.

Böckmann, Aquinata. *From the Tools of Good Works to the Heart of Humility.* Collegeville, MN: Liturgical Press, 2017.

———. *A Listening Community: A Commentary on the Prologue and Chapters 1–3 of Benedict's Rule.* Translated by Matilda Handl and Marianne Burkhard. Edited by Marianne Burkhard. Collegeville, MN: Liturgical Press, 2015.

Bonhoeffer, Dietrich. *Life Together: A Discussion of Christian Fellowship.* Translated by John W. Doberstein. New York: Harper and Row, 1954.

Boo, Mary Richard, and Joan M. Braun. "Emerging from the Shadows: St Scholastica." In *Medieval Women Monastics: Wisdom's Wellsprings,* edited by Miriam Schmitt and Linda Kulzer, 1–11. Collegeville, MN: Liturgical Press, 1996.

Book of Common Prayer. New York: Church Publishing Inc., 1979.

The Book of Discipline of The United Methodist Church. Nashville: The United Methodist Publishing House, 2016.

Borias, A. et al., eds. *Saint Benedict of Nursia: A Way of Wisdom for Today.* Strasbourg: Édition du Signe, 1994.

Brueggemann, Walter. *Living Toward a Vision: Biblical Reflections on Shalom.* Cleveland: United Church Press, 1976.

Casey, Michael. *The Art of Sacred Reading.* Melbourne: Dove, 1995.

———. *Sacred Reading.* Liguori: Triumph Books, 1996.

———. "St. Benedict's Approach to Prayer." *Cistercian Studies* 15 (1980): 327–43.

———. *Truthful Living: Saint Benedict's Teaching on Humility.* Leominster: Gracewing, 2001.

———. *The Undivided Heart: The Western Monastic Approach to Contemplation.* Petersham: St. Bede's Press, 1994.

Chilcote, Paul W. *Active Faith: Resisting 4 Dangerous Ideologies with the Wesleyan Way.* Nashville: Abingdon Press, 2019.

———. *Changed from Glory into Glory: Wesleyan Prayer for Transformation.* Nashville: Upper Room Books, 2005.

———. "Charles Wesley and Christian Practices." *Proceedings of The Charles Wesley Society* 12 (2008): 35–47.

———. "An Early Methodist Community of Women." *Methodist History* 38, no. 4 (July 2000): 219–30.

———. *A Faith That Sings: Biblical Themes in the Lyrical Theology of Charles Wesley.* Eugene, OR: Cascade Books, 2017.

———. *Her Own Story: Autobiographical Portraits of Early Methodist Women.* Nashville: Kingswood Books, 2001.

———. *The Imitation of Christ: Selections Annotated & Explained.* Woodstock, VT: SkyLight Paths, 2012.

———. "The Integral Nature of Worship and Evangelism: Insights from the Wesleyan Tradition." *Asbury Theological Journal* 61, no. 1 (Spring 2006): 7–23.

———. "John and Charles Wesley." In *Christian Theologies of the Sacraments: A Comparative Introduction,* edited by Justin S. Holcomb and David A. Johnson, 272–94. New York: New York University Press, 2017.

———. *The Quest for Love Divine: Select Essays in Wesleyan Theology and Practice.* Eugene, OR: Cascade Books, 2022.

———. *Recapturing the Wesleys' Vision: An Introduction to the Faith of John and Charles Wesley.* Downers Grove, IL: IVP Academic, 2004.

———. *Sheltering with the Psalms: 30 Days of Prayer with Charles Wesley.* Cleveland, TN: Aldersgate Press, 2021.

———. *Singing the Faith: Soundings of Lyrical Theology in the Methodist Tradition.* Nashville: Wesley's Foundery Books, 2020.

———. "Songs of the Heart: Hymn Allusions in the Writings of Early Methodist Women." *Proceedings of the Charles Wesley Society* 5 (1998): 99–114.

———, ed. *The Wesleyan Tradition: A Paradigm for Renewal.* Nashville: Abingdon Press, 2002.

Chittister, Joan. *The Monastery of the Heart: Benedictine Spirituality for Contemporary Seekers.* Goldens Bridge, NY: BlueRidge, 2020.

———. *Wisdom Distilled from the Daily: Living the Rule of St. Benedict Today.* San Francisco: HarperSanFrancisco, 1990.

Clarke, Adam. *Memoirs of the Late Eminent Mrs. Mary Cooper, of London.* Halifax: William Nicholson and Sons, c. 1822.

Coles, Robert. *Dorothy Day: A Radical Devotion.* Boston: Da Capo Press, 1987.

Colvin, Thomas S. "Global Song and Theology: Content." In *Music & Mission*, edited by S T Kimbrough. New York: GBGMusik, 2006.

de Caussade, Jean-Pierre. *The Sacrament of the Present Moment.* Translated by Kitty Muggeridge. San Francisco: HarperSanFrancisco, 1966.

de Sales, Francis. *Introduction to the Devout Life.* New York: Vintage Books, 2002.

———. *The Secret of Sanctity.* Translated by Ella McMahon. New York: Benziger, 1893.

de Waal, Esther. *A Life-Giving Way: A Commentary on the Rule of St. Benedict.* Collegeville, MN: Liturgical Press, 1995.

———. *Living with Contradiction: An Introduction to Benedictine Spirituality.* Harrisburg, PA: Morehouse Publishing, 1997.

———. *Seeking God: The Way of St. Benedict.* Collegeville, MN: Liturgical Press, 1984.

Dean, Eric. *Saint Benedict for the Laity.* Collegeville, MN: Liturgical Press, 1989.

Dumm, Demetrius. *Cherish Christ Above All: The Bible in the Rule of Benedict.* Mahwah, NJ: Paulist Press, 1996.

Eberle, Luke, trans. *Rule of the Master.* Kalamazoo, MI: Cistercian Press, 1977.

Fidanzio, Marcello, ed. *Brother Roger of Taizé: Essential Writings.* Maryknoll, NY: Orbis Books, 2006.

Forest, Jim. *All Is Grace: A Biography of Dorothy Day.* Maryknoll, NY: Orbis Books, 2011.

Fox, Matthew. *The Reinvention of Work: A New Vision of Livelihood for Our Time.* San Francisco: HarperSanFrancisco, 1994.

Fry, Timothy et al, ed. *RB1980: The Rule of St. Benedict in Latin and English with Notes.* Collegeville, MN: Liturgical Press, 1981.

Gregory the Great. *The Dialogues of Gregory the Great. Book Two: Saint Benedict.* Translated by Myra L. Uhlfelder. Indianapolis: Bobbs-Merrill, 1967.

Grün, Anselm. *Benedict of Nursia: His Message for Today.* Translated by Linda M. Maloney. Collegeville, MN: Liturgical Press, 2005.

Harper, Steve. *Prayer and Devotional Life of United Methodists.* Nashville: Abingdon Press, 1999.

Heitzenrater, Richard P. *Wesley and the People Called Methodists.* Nashville: Abingdon Press, 1995.

Hicks, Zac. *Worship by Faith Alone: Thomas Cranmer, The Book of Common Prayer, and the Reformation of Liturgy.* Downers Grove, IL: IVP Academic, 2023.

Hildegard of Bingen. *Symphonia: A Critical Edition of the "Symphonia Armonie Celestium Revelationum" (Symphony of the Harmony of Celestial Revelations).* Edited by Barbara Newman. Ithica, NY: Cornell University Press, 1998.

Holzherr, Georg. *The Rule of Benedict: An Invitation to the Christian Life.* Translated by Mark Thamert. Collegeville, MN: Liturgical Press, 2016.

Isidore of Seville. *Sententiae.* Edited by Thomas Louis Knoebel. New York: The Newman Press, 2018.

Jackson, Thomas, ed. *The Journal of the Rev. Charles Wesley, M.A.* 2 vols. London: Wesleyan Methodist Book-room, 1849.

Kardong, Terence. "Benedict's Peaceable Kingdom." *Benedictines* 21, no. 1 (1966): 17–26.

Kimbrough, S T, Jr. "Directions of Interpretation in Charles Wesley's Psalm Poetry." *Proceedings of The Charles Wesley Society* 16 (2012): 29–59.

———. *A Heart to Praise My God.* Nashville: Abingdon Press, 1996.

———. *Lost in Wonder.* Nashville: The Upper Room, 1987.

Macchia, Stephen A. *Crafting a Rule of Life: An Invitation to a Well-Ordered Life.* Downers Grove, IL: IVP Books, 2012.

Marquardt, Manfred. *John Wesley's Social Ethics: Praxis and Principle.* Translated by John E. Steely and W. Stephen Gunter. Nashville: Abingdon Press, 1992.

Matera, Frank J. *Praying the Psalms in the Voice of Christ: A Christological Reading of the Psalms in the Liturgy of the Hours.* Collegeville, MN: Liturgical Press, 2023.

McElrath, Hugh T. "The Hymnbook as a Compendium of Theology," *Review and Expositor* 87 (1990): 11–31.

Meisel, Anthony C., and M. L. del Mastro, trans. *The Rule of St. Benedict.* New York: Doubleday, 1975.

Merton, Thomas. *A Thomas Merton Reader.* New York: Harcourt, Brace & World, 1961.

———. *12 Degrees of Humility.* Chevy Chase, MD: Now You Know Media, 2012.

Moltmann, Jürgen. *Ethics of Hope.* Translated by Margaret Kohl. Minneapolis: Fortress Press, 2012.

———. *Theology of Hope.* Translated by James W. Leitch. London: SCM Press, 1967.

Moore, Henry, ed. *The Life of Mrs. Mary Fletcher.* London: J. Kershaw, 1824.

Morello, Sam Anthony. *Lectio Divina and the Practice of Teresian Prayer.* Washington, DC: ICS Publications, 1994.

Newport, Kenneth G. C., ed. *The Sermons of Charles Wesley.* Oxford: Oxford University Press, 2001.

Norris, Kathleen. *The Cloister Walk*. New York: Riverhead Books, 1996.

Nouwen, Henri J. M. *Reaching Out: The Three Movements of the Spiritual Life*. New York: Doubleday & Co., 1975.

Otto, Rudolf. *The Idea of the Holy*. Oxford: Oxford University Press, 1923.

Painter, Christine Valters. *Lectio Divina—The Sacred Art: Transforming Words & Images into Heart-Centered Prayer*. Woodstock, VT: SkyLight Paths, 2011.

Palmer, Parker. *The Active Life: Wisdom for Work, Creativity, and Caring*. San Francisco: HarperSanFrancisco, 1991.

Paul VI (Pope). *Lumen Gentium: The Dogmatic Constitution on the Church*. New York: Pauline Books, 1965.

Pennington, M. Basil. *Lectio Divina: Renewing the Ancient Practice of Praying the Scriptures*. New York: Crossroad, 1998.

———. Basil. *Lessons from the Monastery That Touch Your Life*. Mahwah, NJ: Paulist Press, 1994.

Peterson, Eugene H. *Eat This Book: A Conversation in the Art of Spiritual Reading*. Grand Rapids: Eerdmans, 2006.

Pipe, John. "Memoir of Miss Isabella Wilson." *Wesleyan Methodist Magazine* 31 (1808): 562–67.

Pohl, Christine D. *Making Room: Recovering Hospitality as a Christian Tradition*. Grand Rapids: Wm. B. Eerdmans, 1999.

Rack, Henry D. *Reasonable Enthusiast*, rev. ed. London: Epworth Press, 2003.

Rattenbury, J. Ernest. *The Eucharistic Hymns of John and Charles Wesley*. London: Epworth Press, 1948.

———. *The Evangelical Doctrines of Charles Wesley's Hymns*. London: Epworth, 1941.

Ritger, Kate E., and Michael Kwatera, eds. *Prayer in All Things: A Saint Benedict's—Saint John's Prayer Book*. Collegeville, MN: Liturgical Press, 2004.

Robinson, David. *Ancient Paths: Discover Christian Formation the Benedictine Way*. Brewster, MA: Paraclete Press, 2010.

Rogers, Carl E., and Richard E. Farson. *Active Listening*. Mansfield Centre, CT: Martino Publishing, 2015.

160

Rogers, Hester Ann. *An Account of the Experience of Hester Ann Rogers.* New York: Hunt & Eaton, 1893.

Sanctification in the Benedictine and Wesleyan Traditions: A World Ecumenical Conference, July 7–10, 1994. Wilmore, KY: First Fruits Press, 2015.

Scheiba, Manuela. "Learning to Pray: A Journey Through Benedict's Chapter on Humility." *The American Benedictine Review* 64, no. 2 (June 2013): 118–37.

Shawchuck, Norman, and Rueben P. Job, eds. *A Guide to Prayer for All Who Seek God.* Nashville: Upper Room Books, 2003.

Smith, Kenneth L., and Ira G. Zepp Jr. *Search for the Beloved Community: The Thinking of Martin Luther King, Jr.* Valley Forge: Judson Press, 1974.

Soelle, Dorothy, and Shirley Cloyes. *To Work and to Live.* Philadelphia: Fortress Press, 1984.

Steindl-Rast, David. *The Music of Silence: Entering the Sacred Space of Monastic Experience.* San Francisco: HarperSanFrancisco, 1995.

Stewart, Columba. *Prayer and Community: The Benedictine Tradition.* Maryknoll, NY: Orbis Books, 1998.

Sutera, Judith, trans. *St. Benedict's Rule: An Inclusive Translation.* Collegeville, MN: Liturgical Press, 2021.

Taft, Robert. *The Liturgy of the Hours in East and West: The Origins of the Divine Office and Its Meaning for Today.* 2nd rev. ed. Collegeville, MN: Liturgical Press, 1993.

Terkel, Studs. *Working.* New York: Pantheon Books, 1972.

Thurman, Howard. *Deep River: The Negro Spiritual Speaks Life and Death.* Richmond, IN: Friends United Press, 1975.

Tomaine, Jane, ed. *The Rule of Benedict: Christian Monastic Wisdom for Daily Living.* Nashville: SkyLight Paths, 2016.

The United Methodist Hymnal. Nashville: The United Methodist Publishing House, 1989.

Vermeiren, Korneel. *Praying with Benedict: Prayer in the Rule of St. Benedict.* Translated by Richard Yeo. Spencer, MA: Cistercian Publications, 1999.

Vest, Norvene. *Friend of the Soul: A Benedictine Spirituality of Work.* Boston: Cowley Publications, 1997.

———. *Preferring Christ: A Devotional Commentary on the Rule of Saint Benedict.* New York: Morehouse Publishing, 2004.

Volf, Miroslav. *Work in the Spirit: Toward a Theology of Work.* Oxford: Oxford University Press, 1991.

Wainwright, Geoffrey. *Doxology: The Praise of God in Worship, Doctrine, and Life.* New York: Oxford University Press, 1980.

———. *"Ora et Labora:* Benedictines and Wesleyans at Prayer and at Work." In *Saint Brigid of Kildare: Methodist—Benedictine Consultation.* Occasional Papers #2. Edited by Michael G. Cartwright, 9–22. Nashville: Upper Room, 2006.

Watson, Kevin M. *The Class Meeting: Reclaiming a Forgotten (and Essential) Small Group Experience.* Wilmore, KY: Seedbed, 2014.

Watson, Kevin M., and Scott T. Kisker. *The Band Meeting: Rediscovering Relational Discipleship in Transformational Community.* Franklin, TN: Seedbed, 2017.

Wesley, Charles. *Hymns and Sacred Poems.* 2 vols. Bristol: Farley, 1749.

———. *Hymns for Children.* Bristol: Farley, 1763.

———. *Hymns for the Nativity of Our Lord.* London: Strahan, 1745.

———. *Hymns for Those that Seek and Those that Have Redemption in the Blood of Jesus Christ.* London: Strahan, 1747.

———. *Hymns on the Trinity.* Bristol: Pine, 1767.

———. *The Journal of the Rev. Charles Wesley, M.A.* 2 vols. Edited by Thomas Jackson. Kansas City: Beacon Hill Press, 1980.

———. MS Acts.

———. MS Funeral Hymns.

———. *Short Hymns on Select Passages of the Holy Scriptures.* 2 vols. Bristol: Farley, 1762.

Wesley, John. *A Christian Library.* 50 vols. Bristol: Felix Farley, 1749–55.

———. *A Plain Account of Christian Perfection.* Edited by Paul W. Chilcote and Randy L. Maddox. Kansas City: Beacon Hill Press, 2015.

———. *The Works of John Wesley.* Edited by Albert C. Outler. Vol. 1, *Sermons I, 1–33.* Nashville: Abingdon Press, 1984.

————. *The Works of John Wesley.* Edited by Albert C. Outler. Vol. 2, *Sermons II*, 34–70. Nashville: Abingdon Press, 1985.

————. *The Works of John Wesley.* Edited by Albert C. Outler. Vol. 3, *Sermons III*, 71–114. Nashville: Abingdon Press, 1986.

————. *The Works of John Wesley.* Edited by Franz Hildebrandt and Oliver A. Beckerlegge. Vol. 7, *A Collection of Hymns for the Use of the People Called Methodists.* Nashville: Abingdon Press, 1989.

————. *The Works of John Wesley.* Edited by Rupert E. Davies. Vol. 9, *The Methodist Societies. History, Nature, and Design.* Nashville: Abingdon Press, 1989.

————. *The Works of John Wesley.* Edited by Henry D. Rack. Vol. 10, *The Methodist Societies. The Minutes of Conference.* Nashville: Abingdon Press, 2011.

————. *The Works of John Wesley.* Edited by Gerald R. Cragg, 90–91. Vol. 11, *The Appeals to Men of Reason and Religion and Certain Related Open Letters.* Oxford: Clarendon Press, 1975.

————. *The Works of John Wesley.* Edited by Paul W. Chilcote and Kenneth J. Collins. Vol. 13, *Doctrinal and Controversial Treatises II.* Nashville: Abingdon Press, 2013.

————. *The Works of John Wesley.* Edited by W. Reginald Ward and Richard P. Heitzenrater. Vol. 20, *Journal and Diaries III (1743–1754).* Nashville: Abingdon Press, 1991.

————. *The Works of John Wesley.* Edited by W. Reginald Ward and Richard P. Heitzenrater. Vol. 22, *Journal and Diaries, V (1765–1775).* Nashville: Abingdon Press, 1993.

Wesley, John, and Charles Wesley. *Hymns and Sacred Poems.* London: Strahan, 1739.

————. *Hymns and Sacred Poems.* London: Strahan, 1740.

————. *Hymns and Sacred Poems.* Bristol: Farley, 1742.

————. *Hymns and Sacred Poems (1739).* Edited by Paul W. Chilcote. Facsimile ed. Madison, NJ: The Charles Wesley Society, 2007.

————. *Hymns on the Lord's Supper.* Bristol: Farley, 1745.

Westerfield Tucker, Karen. "*Lex Credendi, Lex Canendi*: Noting the Faith of the Church." In *Ecumenical Theology in Worship, Doctrine and Life.* Edited by D. S. Cunningham et al, 40–54. New York: Oxford University Press, 1999.

Wetta, J. Augustine. *Saint Benedict's Twelve-Step Guide to Genuine Self-Esteem*. San Francisco: Ignatian Press, 2017.

Willard, Dallas. *The Divine Conspiracy: Rediscovering Our Hidden Life in God*. San Francisco: HarperSanFrancisco, 1998.

———. *The Great Omission: Reclaiming Jesus's Essential Teachings on Discipleship*. New York: HarperOne, 2006.

———. *Renovation of the Heart: Putting on the Character of Christ*. Colorado Springs: NavPress, 2002.

Worthington, John. *The Great Duty of Self-Resignation to the Divine Will*. Farmington Hills, MI: Gale ECCO Print Editions, 2010.

Digital Resources

"Benedictine Oblates." http://www.archive.osb.org/obl/intro.html.

"Benedictine Tradition." St. Vincent College. https://www.stvincent.edu/meet-saint-vincent/benedictine-tradition.html.

Burke, Adrian. "Prayerful Moderation." *Echoes from the Bell Tower* (blog). St. Meinrad Archabbey, June 2, 2022. https://www.saintmeinrad.edu/seminary-blog/echoes-from-the-bell-tower/prayerful-moderation/.

Cary-Elwes, Columba. "Letter and Spirit: St. Benedict's Rule for Our Times." *The Way* 40 (1981 Supplement): 15. https://www.theway.org.uk/Back/s040Elwes1.pdf.

Day, Dorothy. "The Scandal of the Works of Mercy." *Commonweal*. November 4, 1949. https://www.commonwealmagazine.org/scandal-works-mercy.

Diekenga, I. E. "We Are Building Ev'ry Day." https://hymnary.org/text/we_are_building_every_day_in_a_good_or_e.

Edwards, Luke. "*Lectio Vicinitas*: Opening Your Eyes to Seeing Your Community as God Sees It." *Fresh Expressions*. https://freshexpressions.com/2019/09/30/lectio-vicinitas-open-your-eyes-to-seeing-your-community-as-god-sees-it.

"Faith, Work, Prayer." *The Dorothy Day Guild*. November 13, 2013. http://dorothydayguild.org/about-her-life/faith-work-prayer/.

Forest, Jim. "Dorothy Day." *U. S. Catholic: Faith in Real Life.* June 1, 1995. https://uscatholic.org/articles/199507/what-i-learned-about-justice -from-dorothy-day/.

Frost, Robert. "A Group of Poems." *The Atlantic Monthly,* 1915. https:// www.theatlantic.com/magazine/archive/1915/08/a-group-of-poems /306620/.

"Life Lived Abundantly: Benedictine Wisdom from Mount Angel Abbey." https://www.youtube.com/watch?v=LuiVF2pS9Do.

"The Rich Ways of Benedictine Life at Mount Angel." https://www.mount angelabbey.org/monastery/mai/.

"Taizé: That Little Springtime." https://www.giamusic.com/store/resource /taize-that-little-springtime-recording-vhs196.

Wesley, Charles. Published and Manuscript Verse. The Center for Studies in the Wesleyan Tradition, Duke Divinity School. http://divinity.duke .edu/initiatives-centers/cswt/wesley-texts.

Index of References to Benedict's Rule

All entries in this index represent chapters and verses referenced in the narrative from *The Rule of St. Benedict*. Chapter and verse entries follow the convention of "chapter.verse(s)." Individual numbers indicate full chapters referred to in the text.

Index of References to Wesley Works

Entries in this index identify the published or manuscript works of Charles Wesley, John Wesley, and John and Charles Wesley (joint publications) referenced in the narrative. If the work referenced has more than one volume, the appropriate volume is identified in the entry (e.g., Hymns and Sacred Poems [1749.1] indicates volume one of this collection of hymns).

John and Charles Wesley

Index of References to Scripture

Visit **abingdonpress.com/fullest-extra** to find an extra resource for this book:

The Benedictine-Wesleyan way can be used to form new connections with people in a variety of settings, both inside and outside the church. A free, downloadable PDF provides step-by-step help for church leaders who want to teach or lead this new approach in their communities. This free resource is written by Michael Adam Beck.